TO
GOD
BE THE
GLORY

TO
GOD
BE THE
GLORY

Sermons in Honor of
George Arthur Buttrick

Edited by
THEODORE A. GILL

ABINGDON PRESS
NASHVILLE   **NEW YORK**

TO GOD BE THE GLORY

Copyright © 1973 by Abingdon Press

All rights reserved.

Library of Congress Cataloging in Publication Data

Main entry under title: To God be the glory.
    CONTENTS: Stewart, J. S. To God be the
glory!—Robinson, J. A. T. Evil and the God of
love.—Read, D. H. C. News from another network. [etc.]
    1. Sermons, American. 2. Buttrick, George
Arthur, 1892-   I. Buttrick, George Arthur,
1892-   II. Gill, Theodore Alexander, 1920-
ed.
BV4241.T63   252   73-8690
            ISBN 0-687-42233-7

MANUFACTURED   BY   THE   PARTHENON   PRESS   AT
NASHVILLE, TENNESSEE, UNITED STATES OF AMERICA

CONTENTS

Theodore A. Gill   Introduction 7

I. PULPIT PEERS

James S. Stewart: To God Be the Glory! 17
John A. T. Robinson: Evil and the God of Love 26
David H. C. Read: News from Another Network 34
Theodore P. Ferris: On Leaving Home 39
Ganse Little: One Thing I Do 45
Carlyle Marney: Our Present Higher Good 52

II. CAMPUS COLLEAGUES

Douglas V. Steere: The Ultimate Underpinning 65
John C. Bennett: The Radicalism of Jesus 74
Paul Lehmann: Which Way Is Left? 83
Samuel Terrien: A Time to Speak 92
George H. Williams: Creatures of a Creator,
                        Members of a Body, Subjects
                        of a Kingdom 98
Merrill R. Abbey: Christ's Liberating Mandate 109

Walter Harrelson: Resisting and Welcoming the New ... 116
Albert Curry Winn: The Plainest and Simplest Thing
                      in the World 123

III. LISTENERS WHO LEARNED

Frederick Buechner: Air for Two Voices 131
David G. Buttrick: The Commandment Will Not Change . 140
Ernest T. Campbell: Every Battle Isn't Armageddon ... 145
Edward Farley: Boundedness: The Provincialist
                   Capture of the Church of Our
                   Lord and Savior Jesus Christ 152

INTRODUCTION

The Occasion

Theodore A. Gill

We almost missed it altogether. And, not at all coincidentally, at least two of the reasons we nearly missed George Arthur Buttrick's eightieth birthday are among the main reasons for noticing the event.

For there was nothing about Dr. Buttrick at eighty that could have reminded anyone that a ninth decade was about to begin. The international circuit the great preacher-teacher had ridden for more than fifty years circled him through churches and campuses as regularly as ever. The choruses of critical acclaim through which he moved were as loud and enthusiastic as they had been for almost sixty years. At seventy-nine he had accepted an important new professorship. Publication of some of his prayers had just brought into print another part of his finest longtime pastoral creativity. And new books were in the works.

No wonder the great day surprised us. The brains, the force, the artistry for which George Buttrick can be honored most any time were all in such active evidence before the event that no observer could possibly have suspected that an epochal date was anywhere in the offing. All the reasons why he is important to us were being so energetically inhabited by him that no one was even thinking about venerability. When motion is so steady and rangy, milestones are not very significant, and so are not uppermost in the mind of anyone at all.

The other reason we almost missed the event was just as much a main reason for hailing it. Dr. Buttrick's modesty forbade his calling attention to this occasion in his own life (important as eighty must be to anyone who makes it!), just as definitely as that same modesty has always pushed the private person into the shadow of his professional fame.

It was sheer accident that any of the friends and colleagues who contributed to this book had even a day's foreknowledge of the big birthday. George has never called attention to himself. In a day when some other pulpiteers, with only a tithe of his wisdom and grace, were either retaining agents, public relations consultants, and media coaches, or carefully embellishing their own press releases, George Buttrick was letting the truth of his statements (in the depth of which his whole personality was always involved) make its own impact. He thought carefully, wrought beautifully— and stood back, giving truth its own way. His satisfaction has been in the service, not in the attendant attention. Like all true artists, he knows best how close he comes to his own difficult standards; criticism and acclaim are alike interesting, therefore, but almost certainly fall short of his own hard judgment, and so the same person who kept himself at the edge of his own utterance steps clear of any reaction, too.

So it has been, and so it is. This brilliant, urbane, diffident man still moves through the lecturing and preaching tours that make one half-century-long triumphal procession, honor and applause all around ("There he is . . . That's Buttrick . . ."). And, in the midst of the flurry and fuss in auditorium and banquet hall (or the very Presbyterian rustle in the sanctuary), still the slender presence and *triple sec* voice demand attention for what they put forward, and not for themselves.

No wonder the great man's great day almost slipped by unnoticed. And no wonder we want to hail it. It is too rare among us now, such reticence. With public psychological disembowelments mightily in vogue, and a whole "people industry" geared to get our insides out there in plain sight, and many preachers taking the lead in such trendy hara-kiri, how healthy and bracing the cool air of gracious reserve!

Need it be observed that the Buttrick modesty is a world away from that of the poor public figure who has much to be modest about? There is accomplishment enough already in this continuing career for a whole gaggle of braggarts to make capital of, were it theirs.

It all began on March 23, 1892, in Seaham Harbour, Northumberland, England, where George Arthur was born to Tom and Jessie Buttrick. By 1915, George Buttrick had graduated from Lancaster Independent Theological College in Manchester, England, and Victoria University (honors in philosophy). In the same year, he was ordained to the ministry of Christ in the Congregational Church U.S.A., becoming the minister of the First Union Congregational Church in Quincy, Illinois.

After the date of birth, the most important date is June 27, 1916. Then Agnes Gardner and George Buttrick were married: so enter Agnes, the other half of this towering amalgam, half of the loving pair, half of the splendid parentage, half of the professional life, half of the literary production, half of the great career that bears the proud and grateful George's name.

The family names were distributed even-handedly among the three sons, as they joined the family: John Arthur, George Robert, David Gardner. Elegant tradition: the past honored, but without repetition!

After Quincy, there was the First Congregational Church of Rutland, Vermont. Then the First Presbyterian Church of Buffalo, New York. And, in 1927, the Madison Avenue Presbyterian Church in New York City: the community, parish, and pulpit where the name, the word, Buttrick, joined those four or five others in the whole history of the church in America which are recognized in all communions and need no other definition than their pronouncing, no other authority than their invoking. For twenty-eight years at Madison Avenue, the pastoral work was done, the sermons composed and delivered, classes taught (in the parish and at Union Theological Seminary), lecturing and preaching tours begun to churches, colleges, universities, and seminaries around the world. At the same time the minister was thoroughly engaged with the social issues of city, state, and nation. And in the wider church's own life, his statesmanlike attention to the problems and possibilities of the denominations in America earned him election as president of the Federal Council of Churches.

Meanwhile, the books were appearing: *The Parables of Jesus* (Richard R. Smith, Inc., 1931), *Jesus Came Preaching*, the Lyman Beecher Lectures on Preaching (Scribner's, 1931), *The Christian Fact and Modern Doubt* (Scribner's, 1934), *Prayer* (Abingdon Press, 1942), *Christ and Man's Dilemma* (Abingdon Press, 1946), *So We Believe, So We Pray* (Abingdon Press, 1951), *Faith and Education* (Abingdon Press, 1952). In many of these years, the immense labors continued, eventuating in the massive twelve-volume exegetical and expository commentary *The Interpreter's Bible* (Abingdon Press) and the four-volume *Interpreter's Dictionary of the Bible* (Abingdon Press).

And then, in 1955, at an age when many others retire, Dr. Buttrick accepted appointment to the Memorial Church, Harvard University, where he was also Plummer Professor of Christian Morals and Preacher to the University. The shift from New York City to Cambridge was not at all a case of being put out to pasture. It is doubtful whether Memorial Church was ever a livelier or stormier part of the great campus than during the Buttrick years. The University did not overawe the Preacher to the University. The Plummer Professor of Christian Morals went right on making waves, as he always has. The published token of all this is *Sermons Preached at a University Church* (Abingdon, 1959).

Then, retirement: which means, Buttrick-style, seriatim appointment as Henry Emerson Fosdick Visiting Professor at Union Theological Seminary in New York City; lecturer in homiletics at Garrett Theological Seminary in Evanston, Illinois; visiting professor of religion at Davidson College, Davidson, North Carolina; distinguished professor at Vanderbilt Divinity School in Nashville, Tennessee; first occupant of the new professorial Chair of Ecumenical Christianity sponsored by the Baptist, Roman Catholic, and Presbyterian seminaries in Louisville, Kentucky. And still the books: *Christ and History* (Abingdon. 1963), *God, Pain, and Evil* (Abingdon, 1966), *The Beatitudes* (Abingdon, 1968), *The Power of Prayer Today* (World, 1970). Other manuscripts are on the desk today. Just as new classes are to be held, new trips to be taken to new audiences, new congregations. But only from September to May. All the summers, for a long time, have been spent at the Charlevoix house in Michigan. There, in laky, leafy, bookish rustication, the scattered family reunites, fishing gets its happy turn, the community of close friends is enjoyed, a summer sermon is preached—and the stretching, studying, analyzing, imagining, imaging goes on in the mind never in easier command of all its powers.

All the sermons in this book were preached to the glory of God. They were contributed to this special anniversary volume, still to the glory of God, who gave us George Arthur Buttrick.

Each contributor knows the birthday child his own way, each has been affected by the friendship in ways known only to himself, each has proffered a sermon somehow related to that association (whether in agreement or disagreement!). From among the many distinguished friends who might have been asked to contribute, the present list was compiled in the hope that it would represent, in its geographic, vocational, and denominational variety, most of the chapters in Dr. Buttrick's professional life.

Thus, among the preaching luminaries in whose galaxy George Buttrick is a very bright light, there are:

James S. Stewart, preeminent Scottish preacher, and recently retired professor of New Testament at New College, University of Edinburgh.

J. A. T. Robinson, the former Bishop of Woolwich; distinguished New Testament scholar, and presently fellow and Dean of Chapel of Trinity College, Cambridge.

David H. C. Read, distinguished preacher in Scotland and in America; presently minister of the Madison Avenue Presbyterian Church in New York City; NBC radio network preacher.

Theodore P. Ferris, the late rector of Boston's historic Trinity Church, and one of America's ablest preachers.

Ganse Little, noted preacher, especially during his pastorate at the Pasadena Presbyterian Church; also church statesman, especially in the fields of Christian education and national missions.

Carlyle Marney, Baptist preacher and educator, now energetically at home in Interpreter's House, Lake Junaluska, North Carolina.

Representing some of the many campuses on which Dr. Buttrick has taught are:

Douglas V. Steere, Quaker, honored and beloved emeritus professor at Haverford College; a summer neighbor of the Buttricks, and a year-in, year-out colleague of George Buttrick in the pacifist appeal.

John C. Bennett, sometime president of Union Theological Seminary in New York City; scholar and leader in the field of social ethics.

Paul Lehmann, professor of theology at Union Seminary, as he was at Princeton Seminary and at Harvard Divinity Scool.

Samuel Terrien, professor of Old Testament at Union Theological Seminary in New York City.

George H. Williams, church historian, Hollis Professor of Divinity at Harvard Divinity School.

Merrill R. Abbey, professor of homiletics at Garrett Theological Seminary in Evanston, Illinois.

Walter Harrelson, professor of Old Testament and dean of the Vanderbilt Divinity School, Nashville, Tennessee.

Albert Curry Winn, president of the Louisville Presbyterian Seminary in Kentucky.

And writing for all those in generations coming after George Buttrick's, scholars and preachers who had the benefit of his example are:

Frederick Buechner, novelist and teacher, who has written movingly of Dr. Buttrick's unwitting instrumentality in his own religious history.

David G. Buttrick, professor of literature and communication at the Pittsburgh Theological Seminary, in Pennsylvania; Dr. Buttrick's youngest son.

Ernest T. Campbell, minister of New York City's great Riverside Church.

Edward Farley, professor of theology at the Vanderbilt Divinity School in Nashville; a colleague of Dr. Buttrick there.

It were folly for anyone to try to speak for such a group of preachers and teachers, all famous for their ability and readiness to speak for themselves, and all famous (as anyone famed in the literary arts is famous) for the unpredictability of what they say, and how. As editor, however, I will hazard that we few who here represent the many who rejoice in George Buttrick's continuing achievements do have in mind some kindred notions.

Are we not all grateful to him for the reminder, vividly and vitally before us in all his rich maturity, that the scholarly life can be full of both usefulness and delight; that the steps that go down from pulpit to delicate counseling session or feisty civic committee go back up to pulpit, too; that teaching and preaching have everything to do with each other; that real research is obviously a matter of books and family love and concerts and fishing and community campaigns and hospital calls and books again; that the sermon is an art form, and that therein lies its best hope for personal and social effectiveness; that irony can be right at home with earnestness; that humor can flicker over all and by its light show best the hard edge of seriousness; that the long-mined vein of image and metaphor, essential not only to interesting speech but to interesting thinking, has obviously as yet been barely scratched—else how can George be so prodigal with their deploying; that even in our glut of slogans, aphoristic wisdom is not dead; that elegance belongs to us if we will give it room again, remembering how George develops with that very spare line his richness of intimation and allusion?

That is all very higgledy-piggledy. The long life we celebrate goes on loosing its swarm of impressions and influences and bene-fits. Each of us who has come anywhere near it will have his own list of enlightenments and reinforcements that could replace a dozen times every entry in the paragraph above, and without contradicting a one of them, either.

Most important to us all, though, must be the testimony we have in George Arthur Buttrick of what the Christian faith can do in, for, and to one who lets it go all the way. The conviction to which he has given such cerebral statement, the trust to which he has given such compassionate expression, are not just matters of sober head, dutiful heart, and obedient hand. They are a fire in the blood, a burning in the bones. Hence, the excitement of constant creating, the enthusiastic living, delighted discovery, ardent love, joy in the fray. And encouraging, containing all, the peace of what looks from the outside like perfect assurance.

Eighty years are not nearly enough of all that, though a few minutes in its presence can and have made a large difference to many.

So, to you, George, our love, our gratitude, and our urgent re-quest for many more anniversaries of your engagement with life, the world, history, and us.

And to God be the glory.

I
PULPIT PEERS

To God Be the Glory!

James S. Stewart

We have this treasure in earthen vessels, to show that the transcendent power belongs to God and not to us.

—II Cor. 4:7 (RSV)

Here is a contrast of the most dramatic kind: a stark, bewildering incongruity and disproportion. Treasure—in earthen vessels. It is not fitting that anyone should enclose a lovely picture in a tawdry frame, or a priceless jewel in a flimsy box of cardboard, or a royal diadem in a cracked and dingy case in a museum thick with dust. That would clearly be all wrong. Yet this, Paul sees, is precisely what God has done.

There is the startling contrast: on the one side, the magnificence of divine grace; on the other, the worthlessness of the human hearts in which that grace is lodged. Such an immense and shining splendor entrusted to such poor, pathetic, broken instruments. Such an infallible truth committed to very fallible men. Such an amazing gospel committed to such an ordinary church. "We have this treasure in earthen vessels." It is so frightfully incongruous; in fact, it is all wrong! Yet it is God's doing—and so, somehow, it must be right.

Somewhere there must be a reason and a purpose for the shattering discrepancy. Paul searches for that purpose, until suddenly it breaks upon him, luminous and incontrovertible. There is indeed a purpose, and it is this: to show the world that Christianity—with all the triumphs of the faith in individual lives, all the victories of the gospel over life and death and disenchantment and the devil, all the onward march of the mission of the church—to show the world that Christianity cannot ever be accounted for by anything in man or in his institutions, cannot possibly be explained by any human skill or virtue or prowess or ability. For any such explanation, when you consider the human persons actually involved, is manifestly ludicrous and absurd. Hence it follows that the explanation must be in God. "We have this treasure in earthen vessels, to show that the transcendent power belongs to God and not to us." Therefore—to God be the glory!

Let us look, first, at the two opposing factors in this contrast: the treasure, and its common clay container. Then we can consider some of the ways in which men react to the contrast. Finally we will be ready to think about the divine purpose that brings such opposites together.

First, *the treasure.* "We have this treasure." That is Paul's valuation. Is it ours? Do we realize that the gospel, the old familiar gospel, is still—even in a world of space travel and electronic brains —prodigious wealth, the most incomparable of blessings? Or do we look at Paul as at a man rhapsodizing and growing rhetorical about very little?

I know, at any rate, from where Paul borrowed this metaphor. He borrowed it direct from Jesus. Jesus spoke about the fascination of the quest for treasure. He spoke of the dealer in precious stones, who spent his life traveling across land and sea to enrich his collection. According to the story, one day in the diamond market the dealer suddenly sees before him a perfect pearl, wonderful beyond his dreams. At story's end, the dealer sells his whole collection to possess himself of that one priceless jewel. That, said Jesus, is what it means to find the kingdom of God.

Do we believe it? Does religion mean anything like that for us?

Just consider. What does our holy faith offer? The gospel comes to one man, miserably aware that he has lost his grip and broken faith, perhaps beginning to wonder if life is worth living. It comes to such a one, and it says, "Courage! Here is God's renewal, this very day, for you—the past obliterated!" It comes to a woman, weary and out of heart with drudgery and disappointment, fretfulness and anxiety, and it brings incredible good tidings of tension relaxed and strain vanquished by serenity. It comes to this confused, chaotic, bewildered world, and it tells of the entrance into history of a force of immeasurable range which can literally add to life a new dimension, transforming the whole human prospect. No wonder the New Testament throbs with excitement from end to end! No wonder Paul clamors and stammers about "unsearchable riches" and "unspeakable gifts." "We have this treasure."

It was this above all else that made Paul himself a missionary. It was this that drove him tirelessly across the earth, leading him to the great, uproarious cities of the Orient, Ephesus and Corinth and the rest, with their feverish commercialism and their blatant immoralities—the very name Corinth had given currency to a Greek verb which practically meant "to go to the devil." These were now to be the field for the harvest of Christ. The great, frowning mountain ranges of Asia and the hazards of the seas were no barrier to this man, for beyond them were men without Christ; and the western winds were full of supplicating voices summoning him to Corinth, Rome, Spain, and the furthest limits of the world. Always there was that driving sense: "I must declare this thing or die. Necessity is laid upon me: woe is me if I preach not the gospel!"

And to gird the church today for its task of mission and evangelism, what do we need? More modern techniques, no doubt, and more up-to-date methods, more contemporary structures of church life, more brand-new machinery. But basically the need is surely this: a far deeper sense of the riches we possess, a far livelier appropriation of the supernatural, transcendent resources that are always present to faith in a risen Lord. All the springs of missionary power and passion are in these three words: "Jesus, priceless treasure!"

Consider now the other side of the contrast. Turn from the treasure to the container, *the vessel in which it is lodged.*

Take the actual situation there at Corinth. Any discerning citizen of Corinth could have told you that to attempt to launch a new religion into the cosmopolitan secularism of that greatly cultured and sophisticated city, you would require an organization combining the wisdom of a Socratic academy and the luster of an Olympic prestige. And instead of that, God chose this strange thing he called his Corinthian church, this heterogeneous handful of converted slaves and artisans, an unimpressive, impossible-looking lot, a mad, preposterous choice to be the spearhead of a new campaign, not worth a second thought in the eyes of those who really mattered, and less than the dust beneath Caesar's chariot wheels. Paul himself had no illusions about them—"Not many wise men . . . , not many mighty, not many noble, are called"—an odd selection, surely, for God to work with, poor soiled creatures from the slums of sin, painfully ordinary, often bungling and blundering and breaking down in their allegiance. And this (was it not a colossal, ruinous mistake?), this was the chosen vessel for the treasure of the Lord.

So too, perhaps, in our disconsolate moods we look at the church as it exists today. We see its crippling, stupid divisions, its flaws and blunders and complacency, its uninspiring ordinariness. Is this really the instrument for the glory of Christ? Is this "the arm of Christ's strength, the tongue of his Spirit, and the visible token of his presence"?

But Paul's sense of the disparity in things was even more personal than this. He was not looking at that church from the outside. He was looking at himself, less than the least of all God's people in Corinth. In this very letter, he quotes what his fastidious Corinthian critics said about him: "His bodily presence is weak, and his speech contemptible." As much as to say: "We expected someone handsome and godlike, like the athletes of our Isthmian games; someone eloquent and logical, like our supreme masters of rhetoric; but this man, with his insignificant physique and uncouth provincial accent, quite puts us off!"

Such was the incongruity that Corinth saw. But Paul saw an even worse discrepancy, which they had failed to detect. It was not just his handicapped body and broken health that were the earthen vessel, not just the shabby figure and provincial brogue. It was the soul within, the memory-haunted, sin-scarred creature that the flash of Damascus had shown him, on that never-to-be-forgotten day when Jesus had cried, "Saul, Saul, why persecute me? You are crucifying me afresh, putting me to an open shame, crushing the crown of thorns again upon my brow. But now, with my head bleeding and my heart breaking, I have come, Saul, for you,

Saul my persecutor, my son!" And the man had come to himself: "Dear Jesus, divine and despised, royal and rejected Jesus! O miserable me!"

So, in some moods, we look at ourselves. Who am I to be the ambassador of this royal Redeemer? To wear the Christian name before the world? To be a sample and a specimen of what the grace of Christ can do? God pity me, poor earthen vessel, utterly unworthy!

Yet precisely this has been the strange, unlikely story of the. church across the ages: treasure in earthen vessels.

Now before we go on to look at the divine purpose underlying this startling contrast, notice—for this is very significant—*how men react to this incongruity*. They react in different ways.

One man, for example, wants to have the treasure but to leave the earthen vessel: "Give me religion, but not the church. Why should I not develop my own spiritual life and be a perfectly good Christian, without all this stuffiness of an organized society, all the jarring imperfections of an institution with whose defects I have no sympathy and for whose fellowship I feel no need?" So this man, despising the blundering ineptitudes of the human element, stands aloof from the visible church. And so he scorns the thing for which Christ thought it worthwhile to die.

Another man reacts differently. He is so conscious of the earthiness of the vessel that he refuses to believe in the existence of any treasure. "What is the use of talking," he asks, "about unsearchable riches and incalculable resources? That is plainly sham and sophistry and delusion. For can't you see that God, if there were a God, would have been bound to give some more convincing and impressive demonstration of his existence than this thing you point to, this pathetic minority movement you call the church? If there were really a living Christ, conquering and to conquer, how could the world be such a shameful shambles still? Don't ask me to believe in your treasure when you have nothing but an earthen vessel to display. Unsearchable riches? Yes, unsearchable indeed— because they don't exist!" So this second man scathingly reacts, and flings off from religion into skepticism.

A third man reacts in still another way. He sees the disproportion between the treasure and the vessel. But, being a well-meaning Christian, his aim is to reduce the disproportion, to narrow the gap. In other words, he says, "Let us make a vessel that will not be earthy, a container worthy of the treasure. Let us make a church so efficacious that it will represent Christ adequately, strong enough to be equal to its task, confident enough to be commensurate with its world commission. Rise up, and make her great!"

Now, far be it from me to decry strength and efficiency in religion. After all, there is no special grace in feebleness, and no spiritual beatitude for incompetence and muddle.

But (and this is the point) the danger is that we should put our trust in prowess and efficiency, as though the church were to be sufficient for God rather than that God should be sufficient for the church. For when we do that, however mistakenly well-meaning the effort, it is as if we turned out the light and cut off the church's true power at its source.

The Pharisee in the Temple was a very model of religious strength and efficiency: his religion was really most impressive. But the true church was not there, in that man's bold, brash confidence before God. It was in the uneasy conscience and stammering contrition of the publican, who bowed his head and repented in dust and ashes.

The fact we have to recognize and reckon with is that the church's strength is never going to be equal to the task. Thank God for that: the very fact that there is such a frightening disparity is the hidden secret of the church's power. God forbid we should be misled by the naïve and callow supposition that when the church becomes great and imposing the kingdom of heaven is coming near. You have only to read history to know that that is not true. If God's kingdom is not of this world, then a self-sufficient church would be the ultimate blasphemy.

Men once thought they could erect a church so imposing that its top would reach to heaven. But God flung down that tower of Babel and scattered across the earth those who had tried to build it. And perhaps even today we still need to hear Jeremiah's cry: "Take away her battlements; for they are not the Lord's!"

But now look at this. There is a fourth attitude, different from all these. And this is where our text resolves the paradox. There is another attitude: to recognize a divine purpose in the disparity between the treasure and the vessel. *The incongruity is intended.* The treasure has been put into an earthen vessel, not by mistake, not because nothing better was available. It has been put there deliberately, by preference, of set purpose. It is upon human weakness, not human strength, that God chooses to build his kingdom.

When D. L. Moody first went to Birmingham, that great Nonconformist leader Dr. R. W. Dale of Carr's Lane Church went to the mission meetings night after night, watching with critical eye the methods and mannerisms of this new missioner. Eventually he went to the evangelist and said, "Moody, I have seen this mission of yours, and have come to the conclusion that it is truly of God. I'll tell you why. It is because I can see no possible relation between you personally and the results your mission is achieving. Therefore, it must be of God." Very frank—but very true!

Is it not a great thing to know that God can use us, not merely in spite of our disqualifying infirmities, but precisely because of them? Yes, and that God can use the church best when it stops aiming at prosperity and prestige, stops being infected by the world's ideas of what constitutes greatness and success, stops wanting to be strong (as the world counts strength) hoping to use that strength to build a kingdom for Christ; that God can use the church best when by a great act of faith it will offer to him precisely its weakness, its ordinariness, its utter helplessness, saying, "Lord, take this earthen vessel, and let the world see that all the excellency of the power is of thee, and not of us"?

I confess that the more I think of this the more it thrills me. We are so apt to say dejectedly, "God can't use me: that is obvious. I am not clever enough, not spiritual enough. There are days when my heart is as cold and dead as a stone. Lord, get someone else." And so we settle down in inertia and futility. But if this word of the Lord is true, you must never say that. For, do you not see, what you feel to be your weakness can be for God's purpose your truest strength. Certainly it is only this that makes the Christian ministry possible. Do you think that I, or the next man, or anyone, would dare to stand in a pulpit and try to speak about the meaning of the world and life and death and eternity, if it were not that God has promised to make his presence known through the most broken, stumbling words? And that applies not only to the ministry: it applies equally across the whole range of Christian life. It is precisely our felt weakness and self-distrust and baffling inhibitions, our feeling, "Who am I to bear the Christian name before men?" —it is precisely this to which the promise of creative grace is given, "to show that the transcendent power belongs to God and not to us."

I repeat: this ought to thrill you. For you must see that if this is true, then the church that believes it can be irresistible anywhere, and the individual Christian who understands it is undefeatable. You obviously cannot defeat a man who takes his very weakness and, at God's own request, offers that to be God's weapon. There is no answer to that strategy. It is invincible.

This Corinthian church ought to have been, humanly speaking, in a chronic state of gloom and depression; "offscourings of the earth" they were called. Yet just because of that, it rang with triumph. To God be the glory!

And if one day I am feeling at the end of my tether, disappointed and defeated and terribly unlike the Christ who has commissioned me to be his witness, then that very experience, by emptying me of self, gives God a chance to fill me, and lays me open to resources which in my strongest hours I could never have developed. In fact, it is when you have sunk right down to rock bottom that you suddenly find you have struck the Rock of Ages. And then men begin to take knowledge of you, that you have been with Jesus.

What, then, are we to say to these things? It does not matter how poor and unworthy you feel yourself to be, how dreadfully earthen the vessel, as long as you have the treasure. This is the question I leave with you now, as I would leave it with my own soul: Do we have it? And if not, will we ask for it? "How much more will your heavenly Father give the Holy Spirit to them who ask him?" Is our faith a belief in a vague abstraction called "a Christian life," or is it the living treasure, a sure hold on an unchanging reality beyond this changing world, a passionate adherence to Jesus, and an endless gratitude?

May the dear Savior of us all, risen and alive and most certainly here at this moment, do this great thing in us and for us. The blessing shall be ours—and to God be the glory!

Evil and the God of Love

John A. T. Robinson

God who searches our inmost being knows what the Spirit means, because he pleads for God's people in God's own way; and in everything, as we know, he co-operates for good with those who love God.

—Rom. 8:27–28 (NEB)

Shortly after the Aberfan pit disaster in South Wales there happened to be a meeting of the Assembly of the Church of England. One of my fellow proctors overheard the remark of a charlady at Church House: "They've come up to see what they can do for God." You may smile, but still this is the public reaction in times of war or disaster. God gets his round of a bad press: How can he allow this—if he is both good and all-powerful? And Christians are supposed to be the counsel for his defense. It's up to us to justify the ways of God to man, to show how it's all in the plan, that everything is meant, however inscrutable his ways.

It's incredible to me that Christians have allowed themselves to be put in this box, without protest (echoing the words of J. Alfred Prufrock) that "that is not what we meant at all." For not only do I not want to defend such a God: if he existed he would be the very devil. The protest of the atheist is fully justified. Any human planner who forsaw (let alone intended) the slide of a coal-tip would·evacuate the area beforehand. Indeed, it was the charge of negligence against the Coal Board that it didn't do precisely this. To believe in a God who deliberately allowed it to happen when he could have prevented it is morally intolerable, and no amount of juggling to show how it was or might all have been for the best can make it otherwise. If this is the problem of evil, then I have no problem, for I have no such belief. But the idea dies hard that this is what Christians are committed to—some Disposer supreme who

26

like a super-computer arranges the lives of every individual, sending some cancer while others get a different packet, a celestial Mikado who sees to it that every accident is no accident but can show how each person who was killed in the collapse of the bridge of San Luis Rey (in Thornton Wilder's brilliantly told story) should have been, and equally that everyone who escaped should have.

I am sorry, but while I can sympathize with those who try this line of defense, I simply cannot believe it. It cannot, I think, be said too strongly that this is a conception of God which we must discard and disown, however much Christians have embraced it in the past and however much atheists and humanists insist that we must embrace it now. For it just does not correspond to anything which I, at any rate, know to be true. I remember having to write a letter to a priest in my diocese whose seventeen-year-old son, on his way to school, was knocked off his bicycle by the rear end of a turning truck, and killed. I felt agonizingly for him. His only boy was exactly the same age as my son, and I could hardly bear to think how I should have been feeling in similar circumstances. But I remember thinking how absolutely frivolous and irrelevant was the question some people ask, "Why did this happen to me?" as if there were some hidden hand at work. Or, "Why did God allow this?" as though one should give up believing in him because of it.

Whatever else was true, this was an accident, a ghastly accident, and the only conceivable culpability was either the driver's or the boy's or probably a bit of both. To bring in some intention on God's part in "permitting" it, let alone "visiting" it on this particular family, is, I believe, sheer blasphemy. And it's exactly the same with the accidents of nature—earthquakes, cancers, and the rest. The idea that there is any intention or plan about their incidence is, I am convinced, again sheer blasphemy. Nowhere in that great meditation on suffering and evil in Romans 8 does St. Paul suggest that these things disclose the purpose of God or that we cannot believe in him because of them. So far from revealing purpose or intention, their chief quality is what St. Paul calls "vanity"— meaningless, purposeless futility. True, he attributes this to Adam's sin, which we cannot, because we know that this random purpose-lessness was in the universe long before man's appearance on earth. But the Genesis myth says that also. It starts with a picture of waste and void, of sheer dark meaningless drifting, and it makes the astonishing statement "In the beginning, in *this* beginning: God." And still at this level, where cells divide and unite (millions of them, millions of times a second) and where some suddenly go berserk and become frighteningly beautiful and we call them cancerous—at this level which goes on the entire time beneath the tiny, tiny pinpoint of consciousness where categories of intentionality become relevant—at this level and in all this: God. These processes are all faces of God—nebulae, earthquakes, sunsets, cancers, tapeworms—some violent, some beautiful, some terrible, yet all subpersonal and not to be judged, one way or the other, by the wholly inappropriate categories of deliberation or purpose. Volcanoes and earthquakes build up to their point and place of eruption as a result of physical processes reaching back millions of years entirely unrelated to who, if anyone, may at that moment be living in their track. To suggest that there is any intention divine or human involved (apart from the consciously accepted risk, say, of living in San Francisco today) is as bad theology as it is geology.

The real point is this: given the meaninglessness, the literal senselessness of it all, which is as much a part of the evolutionary process for the Christian as for the non-Christian, is it possible to refuse to allow this, and a billion other subhuman faces of God, to separate from his face of love? Indeed, has he a face of love? Jung has pointed out that symbolically only one of the four faces of the living creatures round the throne of God in Ezekiel and Revelation is human. And this is a salutary reminder that for the Bible God is in everything and not merely in the obviously purposive, good, and meaningful. Thus Isaiah makes him say,

> I form light and create darkness,
> I make weal and create woe,
> I am the Lord, who do all these things. (Isa. 45:7)

Now if this is understood in terms of intentionality, of God deliberately devising suffering and calamity, he becomes, as I said, a very devil. But it is an insight of profound significance if we can see that none of these things can separate from God because they are not separate from God: for God is in them. The real question, as I indicated, is, How can he possibly be in them *as love*?

The first thing to be recognized is that, in any direct sense, he isn't. They are not loving. They are neutral, or destructive, or, in the case of human wickedness, morally evil—revolting and repulsive. And this is focused for the Christian in the cross of Christ. Nothing apparently could be further from a face of love— as the crosses on each side of his bear out. It is a sense of utterly depersonalizing agony and futility—and that deliberately contrived by cruel and callous men—a scene which cries aloud for the response of Sydney Carter's song "Friday Morning," "It's God I accuse." What is the Christian's response? Not, as in the King James Version's unhappy translation of Romans 8:28, that "all things work together for good to them that love God"—that is to say that, if we can but see it, all things are for the best in the best of all possible worlds, and that therefore they aren't really evil. Nor that God deliberately works things thus by some super-computerized design, as if it were all in the plan. But rather (I am sure the New English Bible has got it right) that "in everything . . . he [the Spirit] co-operates for good with those who love God." That is to say, for those who make the response of love, in every concatenation of circumstances, however pointless, or indeed evil, there is to be met a love capable of transfiguring and liberating even the most baffling and opaque and downright diabolical into meaning and purpose. The problem of evil is not how God can will or allow it (that is not even touched on in Romans 8), but its sinister power to threaten meaninglessness and separation, to sever and to sour, so that, in Sydney Carter's words, we lash out against "the million angels watching, and they never move a wing" and are blinded from seeing God *in* "the carpenter a-hanging on the tree."

For the Christian no more than for anyone else is there purpose or intention in the ravages of a cancer. That is why the whole of

Jesus' ministry is set against such things—or rather, directed to the victory of spirit over them. It is not the cancer or the paralysis, the hemorrhage or the schizophrenia, that represents God's will for persons, but precisely the transcendence of these blind, sub-personal processes, whether by cure or acceptance, in the power and freedom of a truly human life. Yet even at these points God is to be found in them rather than by turning away from them. Love is there to be met, responded to, *and created* through them and out of them. Meaning can be wrested from them, even at the cost of crucifixion. Literally everything can be taken up and trans-formed rather than allowed to build up into dark patches of love-less resentment and senseless futility. This is the saving grace: God is not outside evil any more than he is outside anything else, and the promise to which the men of the New Testament held as a result of what they had seen in Christ is that he "*will* be all in all" *as love.* "We see not yet all things subject," says the Epistle to the Hebrews. "But we see Jesus." In the mass of history and nature as we know it the personal outcome, the reduction of all things to the purposes of spirit, the vanquishing of "vanity" by love, seems utterly remote and obscure. Over most of the processes of what Teilhard de Chardin dared to call this "personalizing" universe it is still waste and void and darkness. But, for the Christian, a light has shone in the darkness, indeed out of the darkness, in the face of Jesus Christ, which the darkness cannot quench. And that, for St. Paul, is the transforming factor. Henceforth "there is nothing in death or life, . . . in the world as it is or the world as it shall be, in the forces of the universe, in heights or depths—nothing in all creation that can separate us from the love of God in Christ Jesus our Lord." And therefore, despite the fact that we ourselves as Christians are still groaning for God to make us fully his sons and set our whole body free, "overwhelming victory is ours."

It would be easy to close on that climax of pulpit oratory. And of course it is much more than pulpit oratory: indeed, it is the New Testament passage above all which I find myself going back to again and again. But on this of all subjects we cannot stay on the mountaintop of transfiguration: we have to come down and wrestle it through and sweat it out with the devils on the plain. And the place where the truest perception of such reality is to be found is likely to be not so much the pulpit as the novel. Read, if you haven't, *The Blood of the Lamb,* written by Peter De Vries, that brilliant *New Yorker* humorist, about the death of his own daughter from leukemia; or Camus' *The Plague*—though both are agonizing protests against the traditional Christian answers. But read, I think, above all Petru Dumitriu's *Incognito.* I have quoted from this book before, both in *But That I Can't Believe!* (the title is taken from the same song of Sydney Carter's) and also in *Exploration into God.* But I make no apology for ending with it again.

It is an account of secular sainthood and makes no claim to be distinctively Christian, though it is obviously deeply influenced by Eastern Orthodox spirituality. Indeed, its very title is significant. It speaks of God dwelling incognito at the heart of all things, revealing himself in and through and despite the corruptions and inhumanities of life in our generation—and in particular those of the Stalinist Communism of the postwar Rumanian revolution with which the author was identified at both the giving and receiving end. I cannot here recount how he comes to the flash of recognition, at a moment of utter degradation and torture, that in the response of love and forgiveness the meaning even of this monstrous universe can disclose itself as something to which, however haltingly and obscurely, he must say, "Thou." It is the ability to take up evil into God and see it transfigured in the process, which is the most striking and most shocking feature of this theology. For Dumitriu no facet of experience can be excluded from the raw material of faith: all things, all events, all persons, are the faces, the incognitos of God:

God is everything. He is also composed of volcanoes, cancerous growths and tapeworms. But if you think that justifies you in jumping into the crater of an active volcano, or wallowing in despair and crime and death, or inoculating yourself with a virus— well, go ahead. You're like a fish that asks, "Do you mean to say God isn't only water, He's dry land as well?" To which the answer is, "Yes, my dear fish, He's dry land as well, but if you go climbing on to dry land you'll be sorry."

It is not required to accept everything as it stands, but rather to "vanquish lethargy" in the seemingly impossible response of love.

> What is difficult is to love the world as it is now, while it is doing what it is doing to me, and causing those nearest to me to suffer, and so many others. What is difficult is to bless the material world which contains the Central Committee and the *Securisti;* to love and pardon them. Even to bless them for they are one of the faces of God, terrifying and sad.

Yet

> If I love the world as it is, I am already changing it: a first frag-ment of the world has been changed, and that is my own heart. Through this first fragment the light of God, His goodness and His love penetrate into the midst of His anger and sorrow and darkness, dispelling them as the smile on a human face dispels the lowered brows and the frowning gaze.
> Nothing is outside God. I have sought to love in as far as may be. I have tried to keep within the radiance of God, as far away as possible from His face of terror. We were not created to live in evil, any more than we can live in the incandescence that is at the heart of every star. Every contact with evil is indissolubly linked with its own chastisement, and God suffers. It is for us to ease His sufferings, to increase His joy and enhance His ecstasy. I made friends in the crowd, at meetings, in the sports stadium and coming out of the cinema, as a rule only for a moment, linked with them by a friendly exchange of words, a smile, a look, even a moment of silence. And in closer contacts my discovery spread slowly but constantly from one person to another, in that dense and secret undergrowth which is wholly composed of personal events.

It is this fellowship of the "secret discipline" of love that constitutes the invisible leaven of the kingdom of God.

For this fellowship, Dumitriu says, no labels are necessary, and any structure kills it. This is essentially a theology of the latent, rather than of the manifest, church. And we should listen to it as that, rather than criticize it for what it is not. There is nothing specifically, let alone exclusively, Christian about it. But there is one explicit reference to Christ on which it is fitting to end:

> It was in that cell, my legs sticky with filth, that I at last came to understand the divinity of Jesus Christ, the most divine of all men, the one who had most deeply and intensely loved, and who had conceived the parable of the lost sheep; the first of a future mankind wherein a mutation of human hearts will in the end cause the Kingdom of God—the Kingdom, Tao, Agarttha—to descend among men.

News from Another Network

David H. C. Read

*He has made known to us his hidden purpose—such was
his will and pleasure determined beforehand in Christ—to
be put into effect when the time was ripe: namely, that the
universe, all in heaven and on earth, might be brought into
a unity in Christ.*

—Eph. 1:9–10 (NEB)

This is one of the most daring, far-ranging, mind-boggling statements in the entire New Testament. It goes beyond the salvation of the individual, our union with God in Christ. It goes beyond the union of a Christian congregation in the Spirit. It goes beyond the worldwide union of all Christians in the Body of Christ. It goes beyond the union of the church militant on earth with the church triumphant in heaven. It even goes beyond the union of the entire human family from the beginning to the end of time. It speaks of nothing less than all creation. For God's plan, says the apostle, is "that the universe, all in heaven and on earth, might be brought into a unity in Christ."

To hear this text is to listen to news from another network than those which bring to us daily the story of what's going on in the world. What's going on? Yes; all those commotions, debates, discoveries, crimes, wars, riots, accidents, entertainments, hurricanes, and political maneuvers. But also, says the Bible, something else, something unseen and decisive. God is at work throughout the entire universe, drawing together not only his church, but the entire human family, but every throbbing element of all creation from the heart of the smallest atom to the motion of the most distant star. Everything is proceeding to its fulfillment, to its culmination at the end of time. Everything is converging toward that climax when the universe will be brought into a unity—and then he adds the almost incredible words, "in Christ."

Is this part of your working creed? Or have you been content with some lesser claim, finding perhaps in Christ and his church an auxiliary in your effort to retain your sanity and find some satisfactions in a world that seems to be spinning into greater danger and confusion propelled by forces that no one seems able to control? When we come together to celebrate and we call a "Worldwide Communion," are we merely comforting ourselves that on this planet where peoples multiply, millions starve, and nations play their games, there are still pockets of Christian believers with whom we can feel some vague sense of unity in Christ? When we repeat in the Creed that Jesus "shall come again to judge both the quick and the dead" do we really mean that he is Lord of the future, the Omega-point—as Teilhard de Chardin put it—to which all creation moves, or do we merely have a sense of repeating a scrap of ancient eschatology? Has someone here already decided that I'm talking about some far-out speculation of that notorious windbag Paul of Tarsus, that has no more relevance than Sinbad the Sailor to the world brought to us by NBC and CBS and ABC?

What's going on in the world? That's the question we are asking, and my point is that for the Christian the answer cannot simply be given in terms of the news media. For too long we have shunted the gospel into the sidings while our eyes are fixed on the secular traffic that roars along the main lines of the world. To put it another way, we have thought of Christ as our refuge for this life and our hope for the next while living as if the only real force at work around us were that which determines the events that shuttle across the television tube. With the new curiosity about the person of Jesus, with that new and unexpected sign among the younger generation—a forefinger uplifted to express their hope in him—the time is ripe for us to recover the full dimension of the gospel and the sense that God is still at work and bringing all creation to its ultimate convergence in Christ.

Let's be quite frank about this and not pretend that Christianity is just an acceptable ethic that makes no claim to a revelation from a transcendent dimension. "He has made known to us his hidden purpose." To know this Christ whom we worship is not just to admire him, or even to experience the joy of communion with him. It is also to have a glimpse of what the Bible dares to call the "hidden purpose" of God. This is something beyond our powers of discovery; but it comes to us with the illumination of our faith in Christ. To our feeble minds and limited imaginations this much, at least, is disclosed: that God Almighty is at work right now in the fulfillment of his purpose, "namely, that the universe, all in heaven and on earth, might be brought into a unity in Christ." That is the news from another network, and that is what we should be hearing, not against, but in and through, the other news that flows upon us from the media.

For we don't tune out the noise of the networks in order to listen to the drumbeat of the Word of God. The prophets and apostles were not men who had withdrawn from the world to a hermit's cave to seek a spiritual refuge from the storm. Elijah tried that once when the news was too much for him, and the Lord simply threw him back again into the place where the action was: "He came thither unto a cave, and lodged there; and, behold, the word of the Lord came to him, and he said unto him, What doest thou here, Elijah?" (It was, if I may interject a personal note, while preaching a sermon on that text that I decided to accept the invitation of this church to minister here in New York City rather than to do a scholarly job in a quiet corner of Scotland. A preacher, you know, sometimes preaches to himself.) The New Testament declarations about the unfailing purposes of God and the victory of Christ were spoken from the cities of the Roman Empire, where the news in the marketplace was of riots and rumors of war, of bandits and police action, of corruption and bribery, of prostitution and pornography, of wage demands and inflation, of political plotting and economic crisis. Do you imagine that the Christians of Ephesus were isolated from all this when they heard this word about the purposes of God to bring the whole universe into a unity in Christ? They heard it all, they heard it perhaps even more acutely than their pagan neighbors. But at the same time they were tuned to this other network, and so they not only were assured that God was still at work in their world but were able to discern in the news those things that belonged to his kingdom.

How about us? Isn't part of what it means to be a Christian these days just having this confidence that this is still God's universe and that he is still at work in and through and behind the events that crash upon us? "He has made known to us his hidden purpose"—well hidden, we often think, as we listen to the news! But he has made it known, and to the ear of faith his purpose sounds through as it did to the men and women of Ephesus. So when next we hear a newscast conclude with the words "Well, that's how it is today . . ." we might silently add, "Not quite—for God was there and the world edged a little nearer to its consummation in Christ." This Christian confidence is not the same as the naïve belief prev-. alent in the church fifty years ago, that we are on an evolutionary escalator moving steadily and inevitably to an earthly utopia called the kingdom of God. The Bible offers no such picture of things to come. It speaks of conflict, of the fearful freedom for men to choose construction or destruction, but it declares that the purpose of God cannot ultimately be frustrated—that he will draw everything into a unity in Christ.

This means for us, as for the Ephesians, that we discern in the events and decisions of our time those things that cooperate with the purposes of God and throw our energies into those movements, however simple and however small, that make for reconciliation and the unifying of mankind in Christ. There is a strange convergence happening today before our eyes. The world is said to be becoming a global village. Anyone can now travel almost anywhere in twenty-four hours. The news media bring distant events before our eyes and ears within a matter of seconds of their occurrence. When a statesman sneezes in Peking someone is listening in Moscow, Paris, and Washington. The student generation, which in my day was still strongly nationalistic in sentiment and appearance, now looks almost identical in the streets of London, Berlin, Amsterdam, or Cairo. There is a new sense of a worldwide desire for peace surging from every corner of a planet that is threatened with extinction from man's carelessness, rapacity, and folly. And the Christian church, in spite of divisions and disasters, is much nearer to being a truly worldwide communion than at any time since the New Testament.

In all of these things we can discern the unifying purposes of God. But in each of them we also discern the possibility of just the opposite. When statesmen can rub shoulders at a moment's notice, they will not necessarily embrace each other as friends. When television brings (with the skill and courage of journalists, photographers, and technicians that we often take for granted) its pictures of warfare, riots, and assault, we may be moved to compassion; we may determine to unite in seeking a cleaner, fairer, and more decent society; but we may also be torn into factions venting their fury on each other. Students who reject war against another nation may declare it on another generation and be equally destructive. The universal longing for peace can be frustrated by the widening gap between the haves and the have-nots of our world.

To meet around the table of our Lord is to be reminded of the news from another network—that this same Jesus who was crucified is risen and is drawing all mankind towards its fulfillment, its unity, its redemption. The bread and wine are here, while the traffic of the city goes by, as symbols of the unaltering purposes of God. But they also enlist us, as we partake together with millions in every land today, on the side of everything that makes for compassion, humanity, justice, harmony, reconciliation, and peace. And, in a mysterious way, right here as we listen to the news from another network, we have the joy of knowing that this is the winning side.

On Leaving Home

Theodore P. Ferris

Father, I have sinned against heaven, and in thy sight, and am no more worthy to be called thy son.

—*Luke 15:21*

Listen to those words. That is what a wayward son said when he came home after a rather rough trip. Surely you remember the circumstances; and even though people don't read the Bible as much today as they once did, most of you recognize that as a line from the parable of the prodigal son.

It was said by the younger of two brothers. He was the one who wanted to get away from home, to try his own wings. He wanted to live his own life, he wanted to be dependent upon no one, to be responsible to no one; he didn't want anyone around who would say, "Don't do that"; or even, "I wouldn't do that if I were you." He wanted to make his own decisions; he wanted to come and go as he pleased.

His father was wise. He didn't try to stop him; he knew he couldn't even if he wanted to. He gave him his share of the inheritance and kissed him good-bye. The boy went just about as far as he could go geographically, and even farther emotionally and psychologically. The story says that he went into a "far country." How far it actually was we have no way of knowing, but he was completely away from home; he broke all the ties. So far as we know, he never wrote a letter home, and never gave his family a passing thought. He lived the way he wanted to live. He gratified his perfectly normal, natural desires to his heart's content, as far as his money would let him; and he was, or thought he was, at last free!

In one way or another, I suppose, at times, if not always, we all want that kind of freedom. At times we all want it; and it isn't always when we are young that we want to be free to live our own life—free from anything like a family, constantly watching over us, caring for us, warning us, loving us; free from public opinion, which is always calling the signals for our behavior; free from rules that we did not make and from regulations that we do not like. We would like to be free from the small community or town where everyone knows exactly where we are every minute of the day and night, and where everyone we meet has some claim upon us. We would like to get away from that. There are times when we all would like to be free, with no reputation to live up to, and no past to be a slave to, and no responsibilities to be tied to.

Some of us, of course, are like the boy in the story, the younger boy. We break loose; we get an apartment in town, or we get out of town altogether, or we go to Europe, or to Cuba, or to Canada, or wherever it is we may want to go. It isn't the place, and it isn't the distance. That doesn't matter so long as we get away.

Some are more like the older brother. Like him, we stay home. We stand by the family; we do all the right things: at least, we try to. We shoulder all our responsibilities; we don't run wild. We take care of our parents, if that is what is needed. But we don't always enjoy it, and what is more, we sometimes feel that we may have missed something. We look with a kind of wistfulness at other people who have been around a lot more than we have, and we wonder what it would have been like if we had been able to do it.

If we are like that, we may not envy the prodigals, but we surely do hate the sight of them when they come crawling back home. They have had all the fun and we've done all the work! This is one of the times when we would like to shake the whole thing.

Some of us may not be like either of those boys. We are contented where we are, more or less. To be sure, there are ups and downs in life. Sometimes it is better, sometimes not so good, but we are reasonably contented. We love our families most of the time; we're proud of our community, at least in part, and most of the time happy in our work, and we have no desire to get away from home. But we would like to get away from ourselves, get out of our skins, and especially our limitations, our weaknesses; and we would like somehow to break loose from what I, and many other people, call God. That is, we would like to get rid of all our ultimate obligations, the feeling that there is always something that we ought to do; not for our family or anyone near us, necessarily, but just something that makes us feel, "This I must do." We're tired of having to do things.

We have times when we would like to get rid of that nagging feeling of obligation; we would like to go beyond the boundaries that bind us; we chafe, we beat our heads against them. Both sons in the story felt that way, but only one of them broke away, and he is the one who said, "I have sinned," when he went home.

From here on, of course, what I say is my own interpretation of the story; everyone has his own interpretation and they are not all exactly alike. When I hear him say, "I have sinned," I am quite sure that he was not referring to the wild parties that he went to, or to the "riotous living" that he had indulged in. He was referring to his deliberate attempt to break all the ties, to have no commitments, no responsibilities, to have a room, perhaps a whole house, of his own; to have a life of his own, and his all alone. His sin was not wasting his substance in riotous living; his sin, if you think of it as an act, was that he never wrote a letter home. "I've sinned," he said; "I've separated myself from the people who cared most, from those who gave me my life; I have hurt them, and I have got myself into trouble that I cannot possibly get out of by myself."

This, I think, gives us a slight clue as to what a Christian means by sin. Sin is not climbing up on a chair and stealing a cookie, or anything else. Sin is not gambling, or drinking, or lying, or stealing, or even fornicating. These are symptoms of sin, like a boil. A boil is a symptom of a serious infection in the bloodstream. Sin is leaving home without caring, cutting yourself off from the cradle of your existence. Sin is trying to live as though you had no home, no God, no one but yourself to be responsible to or for.

It manifests itself in many different ways: sometimes in pride that can make a man as cold as steel; sometimes in lust which makes him as hot as molten lava; sometimes in indifference that makes him cool as a cucumber; sometimes in that unnatural withdrawal that you see in people—maybe in yourself—into the safety of a chrysalis.

Christianity calls this "original sin." Sometimes I wish it didn't, because it is not understood, and I can easily see why. What it means by calling it original sin is this. It is saying, this has been so from the beginning. Mythologically, Adam was the first man, and Adam was the man who first wanted his own way. Right from the beginning this is what man has done. He has a longing to be "on his own" even though every page of history tells him that he can't.

What Christianity is saying is that this goes deep in human nature, that there is a predisposition in every man and woman to have his or her own way; that there is a list, like the list of a ship, in every human life toward the rocks and reefs of self-centeredness; that there is a tendency in every human being to misuse his freedom. And this is not an acquired tendency—this is what the church means by calling it original sin—this is not an acquired tendency; this is an inherited thing.

This does not mean that we are held responsible for sin once committed by one man named Adam, we know not when. Poor Adam! All the blame has been put on him. It does mean that we are affected by what other human beings have done and are doing.

During the Second World War, for instance, I didn't feel that I was responsible for Hitler's crimes, and yet I knew that I and all my generation breathed the air that he had poisoned, and I also knew that we had helped unconsciously to set the stage which made his satanic role possible. In other words, we felt then, as we perhaps had never felt before, that we were all members of the family, and we all shared the shame and the curse.

This does not mean that a child who dies before he is baptized is damned for sins he never committed. What it does mean is that when a child is born, he comes into the world wonderfully trailing clouds of glory, but also realistically he comes trailing clouds of dust and dirt which have been gathered together by the human race over the ages; that he comes into the world with the weakness as well as the strength that human flesh is heir to, with the natural tendency to self-centeredness and the natural desire to want to live a life of his own in a sense in which no life can ever be lived in this universe. These natural tendencies are the result of illusions, for we are centered first on the sun as the pivot of the solar system, and more ultimately upon the source of our existence, our God. We can separate ourselves from neither.

I said that a child comes with the weakness as well as the strength. A child is born with the will to leave home, which is understandable, and everyone goes through this to a certain extent. Everyone has to go through it in one way or another—the difficulty is that many people go through it at the wrong time and in the wrong way. The other side of the story is that while he has the will to leave home he also has the will to go back home. He has in himself what you might call the homing instinct.

So the prodigal son who wanted to get away from home, and who did, and who wanted to live his own life, and certainly did— he "lived it up"—finally came to himself and went back. His motives were mixed. We know that. He didn't pretend that they weren't. He didn't say that he was going back to his father because he missed him so much. That would have been a lie. He said he was going back because his father's hired servants had plenty to eat, and in the famine-stricken country where he was living he was starving to death, and his friends as well as his money had run out. He was going home because he would be fed there. Sometimes things as elemental as that point us in the right direction.

He came to himself and went back; his motives were mixed, but he knew that no man can live apart from his father. He went back and he ate humble pie. He said, "Father, I have sinned against heaven and in thy sight, and am no more worthy to be called thy son." You remember he did not say what he had planned to say, "Make me one of your hired servants." He didn't get a chance to say that, because his father called the servants and said, "Go out and get the best robe and put it on him; put a ring on his hand, and shoes on his feet; and kill the fatted calf, because he's home."

It was at that moment that he began to know, only began, to be sure, but he began to know what it meant to have a father and to be a son.

I am not going to drive home any lessons from this. I hope that I have helped you to think about what we are like. We try our wings, we have our flings; then, we turn homeward, not, I hope, as a child returning to the womb, but as an adult returning to the source of his existence, from whom he cannot live apart.

One Thing I Do

Ganse Little

One thing I do . . . I press on toward the goal for the prize of the upward call of God in Christ Jesus.

—Phil. 3:13–14 (RSV)

Leonardo da Vinci wrote, "Man and the intention of his soul are a good painter's paramount objects." The apostle Paul in his letter to fellow Christians in the church at Philippi paints in words the self-portrait of a man in motion, of a man in hot pursuit of the intention of his soul: "One thing I do: I forget what is behind me and stretch out to grasp what is ahead. So I run straight for the goal in order to win the prize: God's call through Christ Jesus into a more abundant life."

First of all, Paul is describing what we would call his "identity crisis." On the road to Damascus (that crucial breakthrough-way in any man's life) he had been brought face-to-face with life's fundamental question: Who am I? What am I up to in life? To whom does my life belong? There and then he found out that in order to master the secret of life which, mark it, includes both how to live and how to die—i.e., how to set up "life-keeping" on a newer and higher plane—he first had to be mastered by some "Lord of life," some personification of the secret of how to live, and how to die, and so how to enter in to a life more abundant.

Paul is saying that the very nature of an identity crisis compels man to decide, to choose between goals: What is the goal of my life? What is the secret and fundamental relationship which creates freedom *for* and security *in* all other relationships, which makes me into a person—a true, authentic person—with a master's degree in living, and in dying?

Paul analyzes his goals, his relationships. Is the first goal, the first relationship, money? Is it prestige of position, whether of race or nation or class or creed? Is it pleasure? Is it obedience to the law imposing an impeccable morality? No, Paul has found out. Because a man must get his own consent to die to any and all of these things upon occasion in order to go beyond and behind them, above and beneath them, and so come to grips with the realities that matter, the realities of love which transcend all these things.

Paul asserts that all this involved for him an act of will based upon faith; he had to take the uncalculated risk! It took a commitment on his part, with no holds barred, to the love of God for all men as Paul had seen such a love at work in Jesus of Nazareth, in Jesus the Christ. Paul says he has seen such love in Jesus' living, and in Jesus' dying, and particularly in Jesus' triumphant living again. Paul has seen it in and for and through men who in turn have put their trust in this kind of love, God's kind of love. So Paul states his own intention: "I propose to be like that, too! I'm a long way from pulling it off now, except in an obviously most imperfect fashion, but I intend with God's help to keep on trying."

He says flatly and finally, "From here on in I run after Jesus Christ—I'm first and foremost a Christ-chaser, that I may know him and the power of his resurrection, and may share in his sufferings, becoming like him in his dying, that if possible I may be raised *from death and through death into the life more abundant.*"

Second, Paul describes his inner discovery that such a choice means a rejection of past goals as no longer offering either adequate freedom for life or security in life for the living and dying required. Such a choice means forgetting what is behind—the good that is no longer good enough, the things I have outgrown, the things that in Christ I have both outlived and outdied, the things I no longer need, the things which I once possessed (and which once too completely possessed me!) but which obviously no longer meet the requirements for the life more abundant.

Paul talks about the source of "righteousness" (*righteousness* is *the* great Pauline word); i.e., about the source of being rightly related to life. He talks about developing the capacity to grow, and to outgrow; to grow up into a life increasingly redeemed and liberated by its God-given capacity to die to the past, and so to become painfully open to newer and larger relationships and truths under God in Christ. Paul says this right relationship to life simply doesn't derive from any internal "goodness" or external track record in "good works." It doesn't depend upon any observable hallmark of body or intellect.

For instance, it is not a matter of being circumcised, as the badge of being the right kind of person in God's sight. Translated for us today, mark it well, it is not first of all a matter of being baptized in order to be an acceptable, authentic person in God's sight. It *is* a matter of being committed to the call to live creatively by learning how to die to the self-centered past with all its false dependence upon position and prestige and perfection of performance. Of that commitment, baptism is an important sign and seal and symbol—but it isn't the "real McCoy" obviously right race in God's sight; of being of the tribe of Benjamin, the right tribe, in the right race; of being a Pharisee, the right class in the right tribe in the right race (how good can you get!); of being a meticulous observer and obeyer of the law—of all of the standards of conventional morality—and therefore obviously a moral hero in the sight of God; of being actively and zealously opposed to all that would threaten these man-made, sacrosanct, and utterly false securities of body, mind, spirit.

If Paul were writing his letter to any of the likes of us today, he would surely say that being a Caucasian, a product of Western culture, a 100 percent American, a capitalist, a Protestant (even Presbyterian, and an elder, a trustee, or a deacon, to boot), an ordained minister of the gospel in the one true faith (mine, of course)—none of this has anything whatsoever to do with being an authentic person in the sight of the God we have come to know in Jesus Christ! How revolutionary can you get?

Indeed (and Paul is dogmatic here), when a man lets himself get to the place where he believes any or all of these things *are* what put him in the right with God and with his fellowmen, *do relate* him in some special kind of saving way to himself or to anybody else in life, *do make* him the kind of person both God and man ought to love and respect—to that precise degree such a man has become guilty of contriving a set of pride-filled, fear-filled self-deceptions which in reality reject the goodness and the love of God. Such a man becomes guilty of the arrogance which forces the Lord of life to undertake anew in every generation the role of God's suffering servant, crucified afresh by such counterfeit goodness, by such self-righteousness. And until a man confesses that this is *the* problem in his world and in his life, the New Testament has nothing savingly relevant to say to him, either in the first or in the twentieth century. Paul concludes, "So I'm done with all that. One thing I now do, I forget what is behind, I reach forth to what is before me. I press on toward the goal that I may win the prize, the prize of God's call in Jesus Christ to grow up—both *in* my living and *through* my dying—into a more abundant life."

Third, such a decision for Paul, and for any man, means taking the uncalculated risk, the risk (come hell or high water) of making a personal commitment in faith to what that man has come to know to be the source and center of his life.

Here we must understand the crucial emphasis Paul places upon the inescapable personal decision a man must make about his life: "One thing *I* do"—not as a Jew, or a Pharisee, or a paragon of the virtues, or a self-appointed defender of old bottles against the explosive infiltration of new wines, i.e., not as a *religious* man. Rather as a *man,* hopefully, partially, imperfectly in Christ, I now take my stand, and speak my piece, and run with patience the race set before me by reason of my personal commitment to the goal of growing—up and out and on—after the pattern and by the grace of the Lord of life!

The urgent decision of life which is set before every individual in every generation can be succinctly put in a New Testament paraphrase of Joshua's sharp exhortation to ancient Israel: "Choose you this day whom you will serve—if God-in-Jesus-Christ be God, then follow him." A man must make up his own mind what such a commitment means to him, but he cannot dodge or duck, defer or refer to another his responsibility to decide for or against God in Christ, and what this means for him.

Inevitably at this point there comes to mind one of the great

plays of the twentieth or any other century: *A Man for All Seasons.*
In his play about Thomas More (the first lay chancellor of England
under Henry VIII) Robert Bolt, the author, wants us all to recognize that a man is free and responsible under God to make the
crucial decisions about his own life. B. F. Skinner in our own day
is a leading antagonist of such a thesis. He makes man out to be
what has been described as "a puppet manipulated by psychological
and sociological strings." Thomas More gives the lie to this down-
grading of man's responsible freedom, of man's integrity. He refuses
to back Henry VIII's desire to divorce Catherine and marry Anne
Boleyn; he refuses to sanction his king's break with the Church of
Rome and the setting up of the Church of England as an independent ecclesiastical enterprise. He resigns as chancellor and he refuses to take the oath to Henry as the head of the church. He
defends his action in these words: "For when a man takes an oath
. . . he's holding his own self in his own hands, like water. And if
he opens his fingers then, he needn't hope to find himself again."

Thomas More asserts with Paul, "One thing *I* do." He says of
his refusal to take the oath to Henry, "*I* will not give in because *I*
oppose it—I do—not my pride, not my spleen, nor any other of
my appetites, but *I* do—*I*!" Wanted: men and women who dare
to do their own thinking and who oppose views popular for out-
moded reasons of conventional morality and urged out of loyalty
to spurious goals.

John Van Zanten comments on the modern relevance of Thomas
More's truly Pauline searching out of the root sources of personal
integrity:

> In the pressure brought upon More to conform to the position
> of the king, we see the dim shadow of the coming totalitarian state
> of the twentieth century. His enemies accuse Sir Thomas of con-
> ceited selfishness. They insist he ought to consider his place "In
> the State! Under the King! In a great native country!" More de-
> fends himself by standing upon his individuality and his self-re-
> spect: "Is it my place to say good to the State's sickness? Can I
> help my King by giving him lies when he asks for truth?" You
> see, it requires a strong man to hold out for the truth he sees when
> such truth is considered unpatriotic!

Finally brought to trial for his treason, More is falsely accused and condemned to death, although he kept his silence to the end. When asked by his judge if he has anything to say, he replies, "I am a dead man. You have your desire of me. What you have hunted me for is not my actions, but the thoughts of my heart. It is a long road you have now opened. For first men will disclaim their hearts and presently they will have no hearts. God help the people whose Statesmen walk your road."

This prophetic word is aimed at thought control, at brainwashing, at subliminal persuasion, and all the other forms of coercion subtly or not too subtly developed to create and enforce conformity. Thomas More of course was beheaded as a high traitor to the king he loved but could not betray by telling lies. He is an authentic tragic hero. His moral strength is the backbone of every nation in every century. He is, indeed, a man for all seasons and for all nations.

In the play, though interestingly enough omitted from the motion picture, the author presents a man easily recognizable by us. Called "The Common Man," he plays many minor roles and comments on the action. He lives by his horse sense and looks out for himself. He is not above accepting a bribe; and he has an easy conscience. After More's execution, The Common Man speaks to us, "I'm still breathing . . . are you breathing, too? . . . It's nice, isn't it? It isn't difficult to keep alive, friends—just don't *make* trouble—or if you must make trouble, make the sort of trouble that's expected. Well, I don't need to tell you that. Good night. If we should bump into one another, recognize me."

Unfortunately, as John Van Zanten concludes, it is only too easy to recognize one another!

But Paul, and Thomas More, each recognized a *priority* in their personal relationships. Each was desperately concerned with saving, with *liberating* human souls, including his own! But how do you really save souls, including your own? By doing one thing: by so speaking and so acting—and *so* interpreting the love of God in Christ—as to help to liberate men from the shackles, material and intellectual and spiritual, which keep them in bondage to pride and to fear, which keep them from being open to the Spirit of God in Jesus Christ and to the more abundant life he brings—

that is, freedom for one another. "This one thing I do."
Alan Paton speaks the trenchant word in his aptly titled book
Instrument of Thy Peace. He writes:

There is no such thing as saving souls unless we save them *for
something*. We cannot save them for God, because they are his
already. But we may save them for some purpose of God. We
may save them by inspiring them, not to belong to God, which they
do already, but to become his instruments, thus making themselves
part of the Divine Creativity that rules this world. If a soul makes
itself part of that, then it is saved. A Christian may believe that
certain of our social arrangements are such as to make it almost
impossible for a man to conceive himself as part of the Divine
Creativity, or to take part in his work, which means, of course,
that he cannot realize himself as a man. If a Christian wishes to
work for the removal of such impediments, then he is not bringing
politics into religion, he is trying to save souls for the purpose for
which they were created.

Such a man will stand with Paul: "One thing I do." Now Christians may, do, and probably must, differ as to the tactics and the
strategy to be employed, but part of the freedom with which Christ
sets us free is so to differ within the body of Christ. There still
remains the one thing to be done by each and every man, individ-
ually as Christians out in the world, together as the Body of Christ
on earth. To take the uncalculated risk; to commit ourselves in
faith to the painful, slow process of learning how to live and how
to die after the pattern of Jesus Christ, that we and all mankind
together may enter into a newness of life more abundant here and
hereafter—this one thing we do. This is the one thing we can give
in exchange for our souls!

Our Present Higher Good

Carlyle Marney

My heart failed me when you said,
"What a train of disaster he has brought on himself!
The root of the trouble lies in him."

—*Job 19:28 (NEB)*

Now that I no longer produce sermons like a weekly run of sausages, you wouldn't believe how involved for me is the process of getting ready to come to you. For you are entitled to a *new,* or an *additional,* or an *advanced* word as to a beloved community. In tons of words I have said it before and better, but now we have moved—all of us.

I've had my five years on Wolf Pen Mountain, waiting for God to say something. (I once thought that if I could get just five days, or five hours, really free, that God would jabber, I reckon.) And now God has had ample time to tell, and I have climbed, sawed, mowed, waited, chopped, shoveled, hoed, hauled, split, built, slept, read, studied, waited, and even prayed.

But God is as silent as he was for Elijah on Horeb. I have no new word.

I am very sad about this; I really had hoped. The inscrutable, mysterious silence has simply pushed me back on resources, people, books, memories, ideals, I already had. I report with candor and regret—no new equipment. Instead, I am pushed back upon stuff that was already said, done, thought, remembered, experienced, and half understood. It's as if God had said all he intends to say until I've heard his last word. Ad interim, my number one joy, life with my dearest, my number two joy, the discovery of church in very small ways and places, my number three joy, the discovery that hearing is better than all the telling I was taught to do.

Does this mean, when I come here, that I am doomed, and you, simply to repeat and condense gruel we have fed each other before? Not at all. If God has not moved—I have!

I

I have moved past and out of my thirty-year preoccupation with man, the unconscious.

It was a good preoccupation, necessary and unendingly helpful. Sigmund Freud, in 1917, precipitated a revolution in anthropology, based on his dictum "The Ego (I) is not master in its own house. The conscious mind is mastered from behind it." My *conscious* and my *rational* must and do give way to a vast, subterranean unconscious; it (personality) is all we have, are, or hope to be; and while it lives sometime in the daylight of the rational or the twilight of the foreconscious, the reality of the nonrational, unrational, irrational, extrarational, and subrational is real, powerful, present, even determinative in the cellar of the unconscious, with a powerful dynamic all its own.

Most of what I have learned, been, and done since 1946 (when I finished with the history of Christian thought as a discipline) rises from taking Freud's dictum seriously. This preoccupation with the inner man led to, was seminal for, all my insights on our inner nature and was totally revolutionary in my casting of an adequate doctrine of man. It meant that over against theology, biblical anthropology, and the history of Christian concepts and cultural values, I had to come to stand hat in hand before a new kind of expert to say, "Correct me my notions of man!"

And this, all this, I have done. I ate the whole thing! Beginning in 1940 with Anton Boisen's, *Exploration of the Inner World,* prodded by Yale's William Lyon Phelps into Dostoevsky's *The Brothers Karamazov* and *Notes from Underground,* I went on to Carl Jung and the discovery that man, always tied to myth, is both myth-bearer and myth-borne. Then to MacNeile Dixon's gorgeous Gifford Lectures, *The Human Situation,* and to John MacMurray, thence to Loren Eiseley, Teilhard de Chardin, and Paul Tournier, coached alongside by a thirty-year devotion to the grand humanity of Karl Menninger.

All of which led to my immersion in group life and the redis-
covery of community—tempered by the awareness of the unconscious cellar drives from underneath, and what the "voices from
behind us" really mean. Indeed, at fifty, blown out of a startlingly
relevant pulpit and parish by physical explosions expressive of
psychic tensions, I have had five years with over 6,000 persons,
980 black, 3,000 female, 1,890 clergy, from 30 denominations, 5
countries, 35 states, all professions—and now I know.

1. There is a cellar set of drives from behind us. Freud is
established! (He must be pleased!) The unconscious is relevant
and determinative.

2. All warped and twisted leaders are warped and twisted by
their warped and twisted loyalty to a warped and twisted leader in
the little battalion of the family.

3. All people revert to the stance they took in their primal
groups when under pressure. (He still acts as a third son in com-
petition with his father and his brothers.)

4. All use transference, diversion, masks, lies, humor, subterfuge, and myths as means of escape from the need to reveal and be
the self. All of us, under pressure, dance imitation dances.

5. Few of us love the self. Almost none of us have a really adequate "I." All of us suffer from some smothering, and none is sure
it's worth all it costs all the time.

6. Many of us have been trapped in an endless round of pseudo-
self-disclosure, exhibitionism, manipulative fondling, an end-on-
end inversion of the self—navel-gazing, or, as Luther calls it,
curvatus in se. And the end of this?

It may well be a kind of health, an experience of community, a
new self-love, understanding, involvement, commitment—and a
kind of undeniable human dignity. Or, tragically enough, the end
may be a kind of exhibitionism, a faddish and destructive procession, group-to-group, of half-born persons hoping for the highly
unlikely. (I know veterans of twenty "groups" who have fallen
off into a kind of escapism; or worse, a sort of invalidism waiting
to be rescued; or worst, a fundamental vampirism which feeds on
the intestinal content of other members, never revealing the self.)

And everywhere, there is an eager, hopeful wanting to jump over the hedges of responsible *humanum*.

Were we criminally wrong? Did we, these thirty years, follow a will-o'-the-wisp? Did we lead the folk into a demonic cul-de-sac where each turned in on each, with a concomitant dissolution of moral social responsibleness, denial of personal and marital commitments, idiotic vacillation toward preadolescently determined kinds of new "commitments"? Did we really abandon what the gospel is about?

I still think not! Rather, we learned, did we not, (1) that "group" is of the essence of humanhood. There is no way from "I" to "thou" that does not add up to an "us-hood." (2) That "church" happens anywhere the group is really such that it is safe to be "me." That the Lord Christ still appears on the road "between" folk: that being Christian, and being human, are the same high-thing; that guilt and insufficiency and self-hate fall away on the road to humanhood, and I can love *me* only as I love *us* and come to see that the us's love me, too. And this is enough to have learned from "the Freud combine," but there is more, a great deal more, a whole lot more. We were wrong, if and when we stopped with inner-declaration and self-revelation. There is more.

II

I have moved out of it and into a new concern with man as responsible agent, able agent, of a higher selfhood.

Whatever you are, you are more than a set of determining and shaping memories and forces. Really now, your parents are away and their voices are impotent. Really now, you are more than a childish and warped loyalty to a warped and twisted leader long abandoned in your romancified past. (You have moved to town! You are a big girl now!) Your memories, real enough, are memories only, and you've work, worth, witness, humanhood, to accomplish in the present. Having orchestrated the "voices from behind" (in twenty groups) there is a "being to be for the future" for you! This task, I am convinced, calls for a higher notion of self, higher than my preoccupation with Freud's (and others') theory of the unconscious can provide.

That is to say, knowing all these things about myself; accepting, no longer afraid of, all these things about myself; coping with all these things about myself, I set out to make (Genesis - Create) something of myself. *Bildung,* a structured form, life, a his-story, a drama, play, an episode. I become consciously directed by that tip of my iceberg that shows best—my conscious self. But the direction I take is deliberately toward the recovery of a set of myths!

We threw away "myth" too soon. We demythologized too fast. For man, myth-bearer and myth-borne always, is as sick when he absolutizes reason as he is insane when he worships unreason. The higher self is available to us only through our immersion in a set of reasonable myths. What a contradiction to where we came in during the forties. But don't you remember? You built your place and your life on a dream.

I referred to *Bildung*—a shaping we must do. It is a merging of myth and the psyche I have found in a Person. It is a blending of memory, experience, and hope in a coping I do with voices from behind me; it is an identifying of my "me," begun in infancy, but now celebrated significantly, in and by and with significant myths I have chosen as *mine.* My dignity and security unconsciously appear. In me something timeless has come into the light, something of value colors my poor little powerful "I," native worth arises out of my life-in-the-group. I build on my flesh and blood something genuine, significant, authentic: a liturgy, a drama, a feast-of-life.

And what are the myths I must buy, or rebuy? What is the composition of the dream I must reify, live out?

Number one is the myth, in spite of all my experience with the unconscious, that *I am* a *conscience:* I really am. Number two is the notion, from Plato or earlier, that will and passion are forces of ego that I direct (this is Paul Tillich's notion of power). Number three is the myth that I am under a law to love! F. D. Maurice and Paul Tillich plainly see this, and in the forties Tillich noted the emergence of a "new form" of Christianity (in the context of a person-in-community-that-I-am). He said it was to be expected and prepared for, but not yet to be named! Let us name it now; let us name it here.

When my power (will and passion) serves my sense of justice (conscience), I am loving. When my love really guides my use of power (will and passion) I serve justice. And when my love and my commitment to justice are rightly connected, I have true power.

Or: when conscience (justice) and will are properly related I really love; when loving and willing go together I am just; and when will and conscience go the same road I have power.

Put all this as the capstone, overlay, dominant feature of my profile, landmark of my landscape, over my acceptance of the pit from which I was dug—and the goal is in sight: humanization, "full-humanization," as Abraham Maslow called it, and what Jesus is comes within my grasp. My highest self is present to me, and all those "others" are fellow diners at a feast. Here, I am home-at-last. I not only like me, I love me, and hence I can love you, good or bad; and the wine and bread of our daily-daily, condiments and ingredients of life-as-feast, in such a company of the glad and the human, become so satisfying that when some distasteful, ungodly, lubricious, and overwhelming outsider like Herod the King sends for me, I can, with total self-assurance, say, as Jesus said, "Go tell that old *she-fox* that I am here at supper today (Jericho); that I shall be here tomorrow, and the next day I go up to Jerusalem!"

III

Given this sense of "I"—this conscience, will, and love based upon an acceptance of the self—it is still not enough. For much has happened to dissipate the person. He cannot make it apart from communion, and community is at a premium here and now.

Indeed, there just may not be here and now a new and confident word, at least no word we have heard. Quite the contrary: all the old words are back onstage, front and center. The old twelfth-century word *acedia,* the word for sloth, not-caring, is but one entry in a whole lexicon of old words come alive in the seventies.

In a short piece so good it angers me because I cannot do so well, Melvin Maddocks catches and condenses the vocabulary of our current-ancient madness. He starts with the masters, Dostoevsky, Conrad, Kafka, Freud, and goes on to Plato, Santayana, and Nietzsche, pointing out that "the new madness has taken the visions in hell of the masters and vulgarized them as *chic*." He continues with David Cooper, R. D. Laing, Norman Brown, William Blake, André Breton, Doris Lessing; but Beckett, Ionesco, and Genet are "old-fashioned," he says, over against the "pop-madness" of Tarot cards, astrology, occultism, drugs, the tragi-comic Satan cults, and the "farthest out" symbol of the madness revolution, which is Charlie Manson, praying to be "dead in the head."

Over against such a backdrop is there a new and confident word to be said?

In this current and presumptous report I have claimed that we can and may have come to the time to pass beyond our thirty-year preoccupation with sorting out the voices from behind us! Significant life and the higher self rest as a possibility on my acceptance of and immersion in a set of rational myths. These myths that I bear and am borne by are conscience, will, and love, on the basis of which I see feel, am, and act out a significant dance-feast-life.

Let me offer as the content of a new and confident word an old and not yet heard word—the myth of a common good.

I can hear you now: "That old saw! That subterfuge of politicians! That old banner of a worn-out Burkeian aristocracy! That chimera Communism fostered and festered over the heads and guts of a billion, four hundred million people! *A common good!* Whom do you kid, friend? That old, dead American dream? That utopian fraud? It's as dead as freshman courses in ethics; as moribund as legal morality. There *is* no common good. Nature won't stand for it!" Maybe so, but . . .

Common good is the myth that made Western civilization a civilization. It's the myth that holds every political, social, economic, and religious entity together west of the Euphrates, west of Abraham, west of God. It is the twenty-five-hundred-year-old driving force behind everything that is worth doing and keeping since the fall of Troy or the end of Darius the Persian. It is the kernel of the German tribal *vrai-doom,* free-dom, upon which every "Western" enterprise, economic to heavenly, is nourished. And, it is the gut-dream of European expansion; it is the justifiable motif of every emigration and every immigration of all the white lemmings of tribal Europe; it is the only justification of all the revolutions, charters, documents, pronouncements, political organizations, and religious bureaucratizations from King John of England to Gandhi of India and Mao of China. It is the great, unrealized, forever elusive, utterly attractive chimera and dream, common desire and longest hope of mankind. It is what all Christendom would have been about if Christendom had ever been Christian. A common good. It is, says Flewelling, the notion without which the sins of our children would long since have accomplished our destruction. But who really talks about it, or takes it seriously anymore?

No one, almost literally no one, except the kind of man who seeks and gets high political office, and what he means by "the common good" is so fragmented as to have dissipated its relevancy and meaning. For by common good the politico means Cosa Nostra: our house, our barrio, our corral, country, precinct, family, club, firm, compound; our boundary, property, values, future; our principals, philosophies, theologies, structures, and institutions; our community, sideboards, prejudices, judgments, and misjudgments. "Our thing," he means, the whole thing, of which and with respect to which we are willing to say to all and any who buy our localisms, "Try it! You'll like it!" but of which our neighbor may say, "I ate the whole thing and I thought I was gonna die!"

I had a different teacher here on this myth of a common good: Arthur Murphy, professional philosopher, chairman at Cornell, Washington, and Texas, lonely California challenger for debate with any of them (Whitehead to Dewey), dead of a liver ailment in his fifties, modest, separated, committed, competent, rare, almost unnoticed in life or death, living on life's simplicities without undue demand for recognition, rank, or reward. No Christian, he said, and hence utterly Christian, he left all he had (home, art, flowers, contracts, lectures, bonds, and copyrights) to the colleague who helped him die, and, among his papers, the best work of his life, a presidential address to the American Philosophy Society meeting in Toronto during the McCarthy sea of troubles—entitled "The Common Good." It's a myth to be recovered lest we die.

But there's something in our way. Says Murphy, we live in a situation of "managed credulity." The atmosphere is politically managed to preserve the emotive efficacy of words that sound or look like reason but will not bear the examination of inquiring minds. So many saviors!

Too, the appeal is always in behalf of shared ideals, common goods, with verbal, emotive enticements, so that the problem becomes how to identify the "ought." Says Murphy, description is not justification, command is not justification, and verbal enticement or promises in a situation of managed credulity are, prima facie, a distortion of the "ought." Because the moral "ought" in a situation is not the "is" of group approval or aversion; because the right is not just dominant opinion, moral authority in service of a common good is not just what most think: "There are few uglier forms of cynicism than that of politicians who, having demoralized the public mind with fear, suspicion, and misrepresentation, then acclaim the result as 'the moral judgment' of the community." But what makes a thing a common good is not what everybody wants when each is concerned to please himself, or when all have been made submissive to the same pressures: "It is the interest that can justify itself as *public* on the terms of equity that apply to all. This distinguishes the ethical agreement that separates a community from a manipulated crowd."

Most of us have lived our lives in a situation of managed credulity where we hardly think at all. Hence genuine agreement on a common good becomes impossible. But real community of intention and purpose, as Josiah Royce insisted, is a community of interpretation. Take away interpretation, in light of a common goal, the attitudes of conscience, will, and love involved, and the action resulting therefrom—and you have no community. Where these processes are interrupted or managed or perverted you have democracy gone crazy and emptied.

On another hand, community in search of a common good for all is characterized by processes of rationally self-controlled behavior, professedly common purposes faithfully served, with pledges kept and hoped-for goods achieved in action together.

Where this happens, Murphy finishes, those who speak the language of a common good do not deceive themselves. The commitment to make our ideals good in action is the only guaranty of the worth of the ideal.

To recover the myth of a common good, we must work with such moral understanding as we have, with men who, like ourselves, are sometimes knaves or fools, within a social process in which the quest for better understanding is faced by unideal obstructions which no amount of well-wishing can remove.

And wherever, in this shared enterprise, we do the best we can—in the service of the best we know, and know what we are doing—there the work for a common good goes forward!

And what do you say to all this? We do have a commitment—commitment in the sense of John MacMurray and Michael Polanyi and Teilhard de Chardin and Richard Niebuhr and Jesus Christ. Our commitment rests on a realizable idea-ideal. It is the crowning idea of a good for all men that would be full humanization, a vast en-manning, a new race of man, a coming of a kingdom of God—and it's a local possibility, if ever we can climb out of our corrals into a truly common quest.

It involves creation, redemption, and consummation; it rests on the myths of conscience, will, and love; love, power, and justice—all in the service of a common good. Apart from some such view of self and selves and society, we are not yet men.

II

CAMPUS
COLLEAGUES

The Ultimate Underpinning

Douglas V. Steere

*I would have fainted if I had not believed to see the goodness
of the Lord in the land of the living.*

—*Psalm 27:13*

An old Quaker once read Gerald Heard's little book called *Training for the Life of the Spirit*. Asked what he thought of it, he con-
fided that for him, at least, it smacked too much of the life of the
spirit. What a different mood we find in the psalmist when this
hard-pressed, back-to-the-wall writer confesses for himself, and for
many of us, "I would have fainted if I had not believed to see the
goodness of the Lord in the land of the living." There is no training
and no straining to be found here, but an utter letting-go to the
underpinning, the ultimate underpinning, that nothing can shake.

Last autumn, we visited among others a brave Christian leader
in South Africa. He belonged to the Christian Institute, a small
group of vulnerable, all-out Christians drawn from all denominations, who, on Christian grounds, have rejected apartheid. This
band of people struggle against heavy odds to stand up for the
rights of nonwhites in that country, and they try to minister to
some of their most crying needs. Most of all they are concerned that
the nonwhites shall know there are some who really care. I asked
this beleaguered man, who has faced every kind of harassment—
telephone calls to his family at all hours of the day and night, tires
slashed, searches and continual surveillance by the security police
—I asked him what signs of hope he saw for a solution to South
Africa's racial problem. He replied that in spite of the little ripples
that stirred here and there, he could see no visible break of real
significance in the bleakness of the situation. I asked him how, if

65

this were true, he was able to bear it and to minister to it as faithfully as I knew him to be doing. His reply that it was only through his eschatological hope could have been almost perfectly rephrased into the psalmist's moving words, "I would have fainted if I had not believed to see the goodness of the Lord in the land of the living."

Alan Paton and Edgar Brookes, two of South Africa's greatest spirits, have lived in almost exactly the same situation and the same mood as the psalmist during the last two decades that I have known them. They do not see their way through, but as Alan Paton once told me, "I live and work a day at a time, and I know that I do not live and work alone." They both know at first hand the ultimate underpinning, and live from it.

Many of us feel a deep discouragement about our national situation: the continuing killing in Indochina; the deep polarization and the slowness of the improvement of the racial situation in our own country; and the general drying up, the ebbing of compassion for the deprived peoples of the world, whose increasingly shrill cries more and more people in this country would like to forget.

Then there is the deep discouragement that many of us feel with ourselves. Who among us has not known what old Dr. Sullivan of Germantown meant when he said, "Have you ever had a moment of awe and glory that has cloven your life asunder and put it together again forever different than it was before?" But what have we done with that? We find ourselves failing, not only failing God but failing other people close to us at critical points by not being open to the fresh hints that this opened life has brought to us. These seeds of concern that in their gentle way keep dropping into our minds: the hints the eternal goodness gives us to call a friend, to visit him, to take him a book, to listen out his troubles, to confirm in him he deepest longings of his own soul.

There is an old tale of two men traveling on a journey together; as they sat in the parlor of an inn where they were spending the night, one man asked the other, "Dost thou love me?" The other replied, "Of course I love you, but why do you ask?" The first man replied, "But how couldst thou love me if thou dost not know what is troubling me?" Within the last month, the seventeen-year-old daughter of one of my friends, troubled apparently by the prospect of the collapse of her parents' marriage, tried to commit suicide. Although I knew there had been strains in the marriage, it was only a week after this incident that I learned, not from my friend but from another, that this incident had happened. It is clear that I had not loved my friend, had not known or been open to know what was really troubling him. Real caring is costly in time and in involvement, and wittingly or unwittingly how often we are not there.

A member of our Quaker meeting was in deep trouble with the culmination in middle age of a lifetime of diabetes and its attendant attrition; she had perhaps a year to live. I recall her telling one of our members who visited her, "Please tell those meeting-members who feel drawn to come to visit me that, much as I love them, I wish they would not come unless they mean it, and expect to come regularly. For at this point in my ebbing life, I only have strength for entering into relationships that I expect will continue!"

There is a lovely story in Saint-Exupéry's beautiful book *The Little Prince* that tells about the fox's conditions for entering into friendship with the little prince:

> The fox gazed at the little prince, for a long time.
> "Please—tame me!" he said.
> "I want to, very much," the little prince replied. "But I have not much time. I have friends to discover, and a great many things to understand."
> "One only understands the things that one tames," said the fox. "Men have no more time to understand anything. They buy things already made at the shops. But there is no shop anywhere where one can buy friendship, and so men have no friends any more. If you want a friend, tame me . . ."
> "What must I do, to tame you?" asked the little prince.
> "You must be very patient," replied the fox. "First you will sit down at a little distance from me—like that—in the grass. I shall look at you out of the corner of my eye, and you will say nothing. Words are the source of misunderstandings. But you will sit a little closer to me, every day . . ."

There is a costly patience and a leisurely, spacious tempo here that does not fit into the world of our overplanned busyness. But the goodness of the Lord that we believe to see in the land of the living—a goodness that gives these hints, these seeds of concern, to those who are truly open—is not really visible or audible to one whose life is geared to our whirl, where we leave one meeting early in order to arrive late at the next.

Listen to the contemporary French priest Michel Quoist, in his *Prayers* where he describes our contemporary worship of St. Vitus:

> Goodbye, sir, excuse me, I haven't time
> I'll come back, I can't wait, I haven't time
> I must end this letter, I haven't time
> I'd love to help you, but I haven't time
>   I can't accept, having no time
>   I can't think, I can't read, I'm swamped, I haven't time
>   I'd like to pray, but I haven't time.
>
> And so all men run after time, Lord.
> They pass through life running-hurried, jostled,
> Overburdened, frantic, and they never get there.
> They haven't time.
>
>   In spite of their efforts, they're still short of time
>   Of a great deal of time.
>   Lord, you must have made a mistake in your calculation
>   There is a big mistake somewhere
>   The hours are too short
>   The days are too short
>   Our lives are too short.

The tragedy of our situation is that our Puritan society for the most part strongly approves of this intense busyness and strenuous work and is suspicious of one who is not addicted to it. In fact it reserves its badges of honor for really busy men and women. In our intensely competitive society, there is almost a fear that if we pause to pray or seek direction, we might be passed or left behind by those who had no such hesitation.

In his *Confessions of a Workaholic,* Wayne Oates tells how hard it has been for him, in middle life, to kick this habit—much harder, he insists, than recovering from addiction to drugs or to alcoholism! In this book he tells how it took two physical breakdowns where the wisdom of the body tried to speak to him and to tell him to slow down. But he thought he was serving God and his fellows as a religious counselor and psychiatrist and really doubted that life in his circle could go on without him. In the book, he tells of dashing through an airport corridor one day at breakneck speed, and pushing by two men who called out to him, "What's your hurry?" He slowed up enough to say, "Washington D.C. plane,". only to have them reply pleasantly, "It's all right, mister; we're your pilots"—and they all roared with laughter.

Robert Frost in one of his poems tells of how many bolts of lightning it required before Benjamin Franklin took the hint, and of how many apples had to fall before Newton took the hint, and he encourages us to realize that the "hints" are perpetually being given, but only open and attentive people get their message and only the unpreoccupied ones respond to the hint. In our somnambulistic condition of dispersed drowse, brought on by overactivity, how obvious it is that the hints that come from "the goodness of the Lord in the land of the living" go unnoticed, or if dimly noticed go unheeded. *Unnoticed* and *unheeded*. "There isn't time, Lord." It reminds us of the line in the book of Kings which tells of the warder's excuse for failing to bring in the prisoner he had been asked to produce. His only reply was, "While I was busy about this and that, he went away."

Many of us are discouraged not only about ourselves, but about our children and about their unconcern and often their outright rejection of us and of our style of life. We are so discouraged that we may be quite unable to get the message. For the first time, perhaps, we can have some sympathy with Admiral Penn, who once commanded Charles I's fleet and whose son had in the 1660s, to his father's horror, been drawn into Quakerism and into rejecting the instruments of war. He was even ready to spend over a year in the Tower of London rather than give up his right to worship in the way his conscience demanded! What a tragedy it would have been for young William Penn, who was later to found the colony of Pennsylvania and to inaugurate a new epoch of religious liberty, if he had yielded to his father's demands! Yet how we can feel for the pain his father suffered.

Imagine the agony of the father of Francis of Assisi at that scene when Francis, in the presence of the bishop and of a large crowd of Assisi citizens, stripped himself of all his clothes and in his nakedness threw them at his father's feet, repudiating any further parental claims upon him, and was taken by the embarrassed Bishop of Assisi under his great cloak until he could get him a rough burlaplike robe of his own. Again, what a tragedy if Francis, who was to renew the faith of the centuries that followed, had yielded to his father's pleas to return to him and to tend his cloth shop in Assisi. Yet how easy it is to understand how that father must have felt.

Perhaps our discouragement as parents may not only make us more hesitant to intervene and more open to the hints, to the messages that are there, but may even help us to understand the Hasidic tale of the Jewish rabbi whose weeping son came in to him from a game of hide-and-go-seek. Asked what had happened, the son explained that he had hidden and that his playmates had not bothered to go to look for him. In this tale, the rabbi drew the boy tenderly into his arms, dried his tears with his handkerchief, and told his son that now perhaps he could begin to understand how God feels who has hidden himself in our world and nobody goes to look for him! We hear again the echo of Quoist's prayer, "There is no time Lord . . . the hours are too short. The days are too short. Our lives are too short" to hunt for you.

Yet out of this self-discouragement, there have come even in our own century the authentic voices that give us clues to lead us back. Leo Tolstoy less than a century ago published a little volume called *Twenty-Three Tales,* which contains the story "How Much Land Does a Man Need?" In it, a man is promised all the land he can walk round between sunup and sundown on a given day. But he must leave his markers at the corners, and be back at the starting point before the sun sets in the sky. So the eager man sets out at sunup and walks furiously to step off as long a side as he can manage in a quarter of the time. He does the same for each side of the tract, and finally staggers across the starting line as the sun goes down—only to fall dead of exhaustion. How much land does a man need? Only six feet by two feet was needed in which to bury him.

Josef Pieper of Münster, in a voice of bell-like clarity, tells us in his essay *Leisure: The Basis of Culture* about the condition of inward spaciousness that is required to receive the hints, the nudges, the inward messages, the seeds of concern, which the goodness of the Lord is seeking to give us. His words are: "It means not being 'busy' but letting things happen." To enter this condition, the only words that I can find are "God's gentling." He gentles us by quietly querying us and our priorities. How much land do we really need? He may even gentle us into a deeper faith and trust in his goodness by a process wonderfully described by May Sarton in her *Plant Dreaming Deep* where she writes: "I begin to understand that for me 'waste' has not come from idleness, but perhaps from pushing myself too hard, from not being idle enough, from listening to the demon who says 'Make haste' . . . . I am helped by Louis Bogare's phrase 'Let life do it,' or by Mean Das saying very quietly 'do you *have* to be right?' " Rainer Maria Rilke too talked of this same gentling inward hand, and about some of the knots that it is well to entrust to God's skillful fingers, when he counsels the kind of trust that interior prayer encourages: "Be patient toward all that is unsolved in your heart. . . . Do not seek answers that cannot be given to you. Because you would not be able to live them, and the point is to live everything. Live the questions now. Perhaps you will gradually, without noticing it, live along some distant day, into the answer."

This kind of trust and openness to life, to the new, to "take it as it comes," makes all that happens have a new significance, and new communications appear all along the way. It is this prayed life, this open life, this life that can observe joyfully the Hebrew proverb that says, "Teach your tongue to say, 'I do not know' "—that is what we are seeking, and that is what heightens our capacity to expect and to be ready.

But back of this kind of trust, in situations where we cannot see the answers or even surmise the outcome, is always the faith of the psalmist: "I would have fainted if I had not believed to see the goodness of the Lord in the land of the living." When Dag Hammarskjöld wrote in his dairy at the turn of the year 1953–54 "For all that has been, thanks. To all that shall be, yes," he was making the same witness to his trust in the goodness of the Lord in the land of the living.

An old friend of mine, Abbot Damasus Winzen, died in July, 1971. His was a life of great influence upon others. He had gone through much suffering and betrayal, and had been tested right down to the core, as I knew so well. A few months before his death, he wrote: "When I look back upon the seventy years of my own life, I see quite clearly that I owe my present inner happiness, my peace, my confidence, and my joy essentially to one fact: I am certain that I am infinitely loved by God!" Here again is the psalmist witness made all over again in 1971.

Mixed with my fellows and with unlimited liability for them, I am called upon to do what God called upon Teresa of Avila to do, namely, to turn over to God my burdens and to take his upon me and get on with the business. I am then to be open for the hints, for the seeds of concern, for the inward biddings that are the business of living and that bind my life to the needs of my time. This means that I must abandon the "results disease," the demand that I do the harvesting and am entitled to keep tab on the weight of the sacks that I have threshed. In terms of hope, Erich Fromm gathers up this self-abandonment in conscious trust to the eternal goodness working in the land of the living: "To hope means at every moment to be ready at every moment for that which is not yet born, and yet not to become desperate if there is no birth in our life time. Those whose hope is weak settle down for comfort or for violence; those whose hope is strong see and cherish all signs of new life and are ready at every moment to help the birth of that which is ready to be born."

Knowing that small things matter; knowing that we are not alone; knowing that we are being given hints that require heeding; but knowing, too, that these hints may come to us only if we are not too "busy" but let things happen, we might close with the words of the old spiritual:

God is so high that you can't get above him
God is so wide that you can't get around him
God is so deep that you can't get beneath him,
So you'd better come in through the gate.

And the bidding says, "Come in, come in, come all the way in."

The Radicalism of Jesus

John C. Bennett

From time to time the question is raised as to whether Jesus was a political revolutionary. In the past few years this question has been raised again with great emphasis. It fits a time when, in many parts of the world, people who have been oppressed for centuries are struggling to bring about revolutionary changes in their condition. Professor S. G. Brandon, in his scholarly *Jesus and the Zealots,* claims that Jesus was a fellow traveler of the Zealots, who were first-century guerrillas opposed to the Roman power in Palestine. The University of Manchester teacher, in order to make his point, has to regard the pacifism in the Sermon on the Mount as an addition to the Gospel record, included to prove to the Roman authorities that the early church was no threat to them, and thus to gain for the church greater toleration.

That last point taxes credulity more than anything else in the author's view of Jesus. It is hard to believe that the Sermon on the Mount was fabricated to put the Romans off guard.

Professor Oscar Cullmann, in his *Jesus and the Revolutionaries,* responds to Professor Brandon by presenting a view that is more in line with the church's conventional interpretations of Jesus. Yet Professor Cullmann's more familiar-sounding statement has a quiet, unfamiliar edge to it. Cullmann does believe that Jesus was attracted by the Zealot cause, that there was a significance in the fact that one of his disciples was called a Zealot, and that he was actually crucified in the mistaken belief that he was a Zealot. However, Cullmann believes that the teaching of Jesus about nonviolence and about love for enemies was authentic. Instead of making a great deal of the strange words of Jesus to his disciples, "Let him who has no sword sell his mantle and buy one," he would have that passage interpreted in the light of others including the saying in which Jesus rebuked his disciples: "Put your sword back into its place; for all who take the sword will perish by the sword."

I said that Cullmann's interpretation has an edge that has often been lacking in similar, more conventional statements of the case reflecting, as they often do, an eagerness to prove that Jesus was not a revolutionary. He does emphasize the profound radicalism and revolutionary spirit in the teachings and acts of Jesus; but he says that Jesus was not a political revolutionary. It is a great relief to many people in the church to be assured that Jesus was not political! In Jesus' own time and place, political action was not a lively possibility for a small minority within a minority of the Roman world. When political violence was tried, it brought only severe repression. Moreover, the role of Jesus was not that of a political messiah, but was that of revealer and redeemer on a deeper level. However, there were aspects of the teachings and examples of Jesus which in another situation should inspire radical political action. It is not to get Christians today off the hook that we say Jesus in his time and in his role was nonpolitical.

Think of the range of the radicalism of Jesus in relation to the dominant attitudes and institutions of his own time.

The story of his appearance in the synagogue in Nazareth tells how he quoted Isaiah, so directing his message to the liberation of the victims of society: the poor, the captives, the blind, the oppressed. By doing so, he made clear the continuity between his message and that of the Old Testament prophets. Also, on that occasion he challenged what we would now call the racism of his hearers when he recalled what Elisha the prophet had done for Gentiles rather than for Jews. And, if it is stretching a point to use the word *racism* here in the contemporary sense, at the very least we have here a case of ethnocentrism, of preference for the "ins" as opposed to the "outs." Jesus touched a nerve that was so sensitive among the people of his own town that they became a mob that tried to destroy him. This was one of several occasions which might have led to a passion before the Passion.

Jesus defied the religious Establishment by healing on the sabbath, saying that "the sabbath was made for man, and not man for the sabbath." What a liberating word this was for the understanding of the relation between institutions and the real welfare of persons. Too often we sacrifice people to institutions out of habit, and never ask why we do it.

At the expense of the priest and the Levite, he praised the hated Samaritan; and in other parables the prodigal son comes off better than the prudent, respectable elder brother, and the despised tax collector is made to look better than the honored Pharisee. All along the line, people who were generally despised were given preference: "The publicans and harlots go into the kingdom of Heaven before you."

He even set the wisdom of children above that of adults.

He distrusted wealth not only because the poor were its victims, but also because the rich were its victims: "It is easier for a camel to go through the eye of a needle than for a rich man to enter the kingdom of God." Yet he did not spiritualize the problem of wealth versus poverty so that the poor in their material misery were neglected. In the story of Dives and Lazarus, Lazarus was full of very nonspiritual sores, and he desired material food from the rich man's table. Above all, in the story of the Last Judgment in Matthew 25 it's those who were literally hungry and thirsty and were literally strangers (we might now say refugees), naked, sick, and in prison, that were the ones in whom God himself was present.

The account of the cleansing of the Temple has much to say to us. It was this event that caused the authorities to seek again to destroy him. Because he had attacked the traders and money-changers in the Temple, we see that his encounter was with the economic powers in his society. He touched another nerve which was very sensitive. His own motive may not have been economic, because he was especially outraged by the defilement of the Temple as the house of God. There is something very modern about this event. When it was said that "he would not allow anyone to use the temple court as a thoroughfare for carrying goods" we are reminded of many a disruptive demonstration against the Vietnam war in our own time, the kind of demonstration that is usually disapproved in the churches today. Whether or not such acts of disruption are counterproductive should be settled by careful calculation, but they should not shock churches.

Sometimes those who stress the nonviolence of Jesus are troubled by this Temple episode, but I think that it fills out the picture of Jesus and shows that he could take strong action against evil. There was no lethal violence here, no precedent for military violence, for the use of napalm, for bombing cities and villages. Also, there is a parallel here to the action of the Berrigans and their friends in entering the office of a draft board and destroying draft files. In that famous case, the force used was no more than pushing, without the intent to injure anyone. In neither case was force used to solve a problem. Probably the traders were back in the Temple the next day—and we know that the draft board was soon functioning again. Instead, each commotion was a symbolic act to call attention to a problem.

Jesus turned upside down the usual human way of understanding authority and greatness when he said to his disciples, "You know that the rulers lord it over them, and their great men exercise authority over them. It shall not be so among you; but whoever would be great among you must be your servant." Jesus in his own life and death demonstrated this understanding of authority and greatness.

Was there any kind of Establishment that Jesus did not challenge? Was there any attitude that leads to injustice and oppression which Jesus did not seek to transform?

This radicalism of Jesus has been tamed in Christian history. In fact, it has generally been totally obscured by the tendency to accent the Christ of dogma or the risen Christ, without asking what clue to the nature of Christ and to the God who acted in him is to be found in the radical teaching and example of the Jesus of the Gospels. Today in the church this question is being asked on many sides. The people who need radical change have gained a voice, and they respond to the radical Jesus; this is also true of the corporate mind of the church, both Catholic and Protestant, when in our time it has faced the dreadful contrast between the rich and the poor in the world.

It has come to be a commonplace of Christian teaching that there is a bias within the Christian view of life in favor of the weak and poor and defenseless. I use the word *bias* because we need to be shocked by it, so that we really see what is involved here. There is a bias in many of the Gospel passages to which I have referred, and it is often regarded as unfair by the rich and the strong and the well-defended. This bias often has political implications offensive to many people in the churches. Several denominations in this country have been badly split when agencies of the denominations made grants of money to black groups within the churches, hoping, in some small way, to make up for the crippling disadvantages from which the blacks in this country have suffered for centuries. These have been only token responses, but they have created fears that the principle of "reparations" which inspired these grants might require more such responses in the future. There was also a sense of unfairness to those who have "made it" on their own.

This bias does not mean that God loves the poor and defenseless more than he does those who have great external advantages. Rather we should think of it as a strategic concentration upon the lost sheep in the Gospel parable. What else but an unfair bias could it seem to the ninety and nine who went not astray, when there was so much joy in heaven over the recovery of one sheep that was lost? One must use this parable guardedly in this context: I do not want to suggest that the poor and defenseless are more lost than others. The contrary is at least as likely.

Karl Barth (who is generally regarded as the greatest Protestant theologian of this century, and who in his basic approach to Christianity is far removed from the liberal social gospel) emphasized this bias, so important today in interpreting the radicalism of Jesus. He says, in one passage suggested by the parable of the lost sheep, that the church must cast all "false impartiality aside"—impartiality, that is, as between the weak and the strong. The church must, he says, have as its chief concern "the poor, the socially and economically weak and threatened," and it must "insist on the

State's special responsibility for these weaker members of society."
In another passage he declares that "God always takes his stand
unconditionally and passionately on this side and on this side alone;
against the lofty and in behalf of the lowly; against those who
already enjoy right and privilege, and on behalf of those who are
denied it and deprived of it."

Pope Paul VI, in his great encyclical *Populorum Progressio* ("On
the Development of the Peoples"), speaks in the same spirit. He
says of the rich nations that unless they share their wealth with
the poor "their continued greed will call down upon them the
judgment of God and the wrath of the poor, with consequences
no one can foretell." This idea of the converging of the judgment
of God and the wrath of the poor is not new, but it comes at this
time with great force from the Pope. Already his encyclical has become the basis on which many Christians in Latin America become involved in revolutionary struggles for liberation from the
power of their own oligarchies and from that of the United States.

One other witness: James Cone, the chief creator of what he
calls "Black Theology," who represents many young Christians,
black Christians especially. He writes about the theme of the liberation of oppressed people as the heart of the Christian message. He
says: "It seems clear that the overwhelming weight of biblical
teaching, especially the prophetic tradition in which Jesus stood
unambiguously, is upon the unqualified identification with the poor
precisely because they are poor." Cone keeps saying that white
theologians cannot fully grasp the meaning of this identification of
Christ with the oppressed, and, while he may exaggerate this point
so far as individuals are concerned, it is only too true of trends in
Christian history.

I think that we can respond best to the radicalism of Jesus as
we come to realize the irony in the fact that the followers of Jesus
became the top people in the richest and most powerful nations in
the world. The Christian religion has been used to sanction the
authority of rulers, no matter how oppressive they have been; it
has been used to justify the claims of wealth; it has been used to
give religious sanction to the pretensions of the empires which, with
their base in "Christendom," have dominated so much of the world.

There is great irony in this, but we need not respond cynically. Rather we should learn from it. There proved to be an extraordinary dynamism in the Christian movement. It had considerable part in the creation of Western civilization. The very success of Christianity in this respect meant that Christians came to be on top of this civilization. There are many debates about the precise influence of aspects of Christianity in the development of capitalism and in the advance of science and technology, but these are in part the result of the history-making elements in Christianity, and are related to the biblical understanding of creation, man, and history. The church did much to discipline and even to sensitize the conscience of humanity, but it also bred moral complacency about the dominant institutions of society; the radicalism of Jesus seldom disturbed the Christian conscience. In 1948 the bishops of the Anglican Communion at the Lambeth Conference admitted this in the following remarkable confession from the leaders of a great church: "The Christian Church through the formative decades of the industrial era showed little insight into what was befalling human society. The Church of England was identified almost completely with the ruling classes as were the churches of central and eastern Europe." They go on to say that "only in more recent times has the church begun to make a radical critique of western society, and to provide a climate not hostile to revolutionary spirits." A similar generalization has been made by one of the most authoritative historians of American Protestantism. Henry F. May says of our American churches in the latter part of the nineteenth century, "In 1876 Protestanism presented a massive, almost unbroken front in its defense of the social *status quo.*"

Today there is a very widespread realization that the regular identification of the Christians with the most powerful and privileged people in the world has greatly distorted the impact of Christianity upon the world. This realization is directly related to the fact that for the first time in history the main-line churches have had to take seriously the calls for liberation, for revolutionary change, from oppressed people on all continents. The peoples of the Third World are now talking back to us who, in the past, expected them to do the listening. In our own country the black people have put white people on the moral defensive as never before.

One striking illustration of how Christians in the rich and powerful nations are addressed now by Christians in the Third World is a word that has come from the Roman Catholic Archbishop Helder Camara in Brazil to Christians in the northern hemisphere. Archbishop Camara is one of the most heroic Christian spirits in the world today, for he risks his freedom and his life daily as he opposes his government, strongly supported as it is by our government. He has said the following to us:

> Our responsibility as Christians makes us tremble. The northern hemisphere, the developed area of the world, the 20 percent who possess 80 percent of the world's resources, are of Christian origin. What impression can our African and Asian brethren and the masses of Latin America have of Christianity, if the tree is to be judged by its fruits? For we Christians are largely responsible for the unjust world in which we live. . . . What a splendid testimony we could give if we were to unite with our Christian brethren in the developed countries to do everything in our power to overcome the egoism of the northern hemisphere—which is the Christian hemisphere or at any rate Christian in origin!

"The egoism of the northern hemisphere"—that is a phrase that is quite new to most of us. It jars us and we are called to listen. We are called to a new and deep probing of what it means to be Christians on top of a world full of poverty and oppression. May we be helped by Christ himself to understand the organized resentments of peoples who need radical change, and to accept new situations for us when other peoples loved by God come into their own.

Response to the radicalism of Jesus often involves political choices in our time and place. There is no sure guidance to such choices, even though we should be led to seek the best answers available. Not only are there conflicts between those who defend old forms of injustice and those who seek the transformation of society, but there are also many conflicts between those who have different roads to such transformation. Sometimes we may be tempted to say, "A plague on *all* your houses," and then try to carve out for ourselves a position of neutrality; but, in practice, neutrality means support of the status quo. Though there are no directives from the New Testament as we try to find our way amidst current complexities and confusions, it will make a vast difference if we will just appreciate the extent of the irony in one fact: the followers of Jesus are often the rich and the powerful in the northern hemisphere. How can we then not grasp the fact that Christianity itself as known to comfortable, white Christians has been distorted? It also will make us see our role differently if we develop a habit of putting the burden of proof on the defenders of present structures of domination.

The radicalism of Jesus is deeper than that of political movements seeking power to change society, though it is no substitute for our choosing among them. There will be radical changes, and the once mighty will lose many kinds of thrones, will be new victims. This does not mean that we are subject to a fate that prevents any gains for justice; it does mean that gains that are achieved will always need to be kept under radical criticism. And changes in structures will never be enough, though they are necessary. The radicalism of Jesus should lead us into a new awareness, into a change of heart, into a new spirit, into a new openness to the continuing judgment of God upon us and upon our society.

Which Way Is Left?

Paul Lehmann

When the Son of Man comes in his glory and all the angels with him, he will sit in state on his throne, with all the nations gathered before him. He will separate men into two groups, as a shepherd separates the sheep from the goats, and he will place the sheep on his right hand and the goats on his left.

—Matt. 25:31–33 (NEB)

Recently I arrived at a college campus to find the students in a state of noisy and bewildering excitement. The occasion for it had been an all-day symposium in which the editor of *Ramparts* magazine, Edward M. Keating, had undertaken to interpret and to defend the "new left." Mr. Keating had come under sharp attack from a democratic-socialist, Tom Kahn, author of *The Accidental Revolution,* and from Professor Philip Rieff of the department of sociology at the University of Pennsylvania.

The editor of *Ramparts* had put forward his own version of the Establishment–anti-Establishment hostilities barely slumbering beneath the surface of society and culture in the United States today. Mr. Keating characterized the Establishment as the "radical middle," and as "the greatest danger that we face today" owing to its attempt to maintain affluence, respectability, and traditional Americanism by means of the politics and morality of the big lie. The illegality of the war in Vietnam was the principal focus of the indictment. Mr. Keating's alternative to the Establishment and all its works was a movement, more moral than political, which he labeled "the community of concern."

The attack upon this attack on the radical middle was a double one. From the political side, the aims of the new left are better served (so Mr. Kahn argued) by a coalition of labor and minority forces seeking to change the structures of power. Mr. Keating's version of the new left was "a surface-level irritant to society which does not go below the surface to heal the cause of irritation." The curse of the new left is that it is "a revolution unmanned by revolutionaries." As a self-styled "academic intellectualist liberal," Professor Rieff tried to lift the new left beyond the impasse between vague humanitarianism and doctrinaire political protest, and to direct attention to the value conflict at the root of the present cultural crisis. As one might expect, a sociologist has his own jargon for analyzing such a value crisis. What concerns us, however, is his proposal that "a social system is a system of values that depends on change, not stability," and that what is called for is new values which can operate as effective demands.

Here, then, was a vigorously debated profile of the new left. It was only one profile—not intended as a general, much less a final, characterization. It turned out as an exploration of a "new world cacophony" which might become a symphony. Somehow, dimly sensing this world as their world and as claiming them, the students came away from this attempt to point directions, with an understandable question which has haunted me ever since. The campus paper headline read "All Day Symposium Speakers Disagree Which Way Is Left."

I. Passion and Pathos

Well, then, which way is left? The question gathers into sound the less and less hollow revolutionary longings of peoples on the move, and echoes insistently across and around the earth—in orbit as well as on the globe. Yet one scarcely knows how to give it proper utterance. Shall we ask, Which way is *left?* How can one put it that way without drifting into a dead-end remainder? When all other possibilities have played themselves out, there is nothing really left.

Suppose we put it this way: Which way *is* left? That seems to get nearer the heart of the matter, for it seems to hint that "left" is a direction which makes sense of further asking. Everything that makes all the difference in the world to the one who cannot suppress the question opens into freedom when that turn has been taken. But here too we must do our own asking with due deliberation. For if we ask, Which way *is* left? too loudly, we may be tempted to exchange our impatience for some short-cut programmatic, ideological, or power reply. Left is where Castroism threatens the dubiously democratic political fruits of the Alliance for Progress with counterrevolutionary resistance. Or, left is what Moscow says Peiping is not and Peiping says that Moscow is not. Or, left is the "where" and the "how" of whatever must be passionately pursued or secretly controlled if the dynamics of underdevelopment are ever to lead to development. Or, left is what keeps the Oder-Neisse line intact, and the balance of power between there and the Atlantic off-balance, until a familiar German dictum about "the continuation of policy by other means" goes well beyond the planning stage. Or, left is what the CIA cryptically spends its cryptic funds trying to provide with a properly bought and delivered conversation partner in international student conferences.

Which brings us back to the editor of *Ramparts* and his antiseptic critics. Which way *is* left, when a community of concern is caught between ideological power solutions and a value crisis, and is dissipated by a passionate distrust of the radical middle? How in such a community can a liberating cause and a fulfilling commitment get together?

Maybe this same question was bugging James Dickey as he pondered two words of E. M. Forster's—"only connect"—and then went on to try to put "Power and Light" together:

I may even be
A man, I tell my wife: all day I climb myself
Bowlegged up those damned poles   rooster-heeled in all
Kinds of weather   and what is there when I get
Home? . . .

            . . . My watch glows with the time to rise
And shine. Never think I don't know my profession
Will lift me: why, all over hell the lights burn in your eyes,
People are calling each other   weeping with a hundred thousand
Volts   making deals   pleading   laughing like fate,
Far off, invulnerable   or with the right word pierced

To the heart

By wires I held, shooting off their ghostly mouths
In my gloves. . . .

                                             . . . I know the secret of sitting
In light   of eating a limp piece of bread   under
The red-veined eyeball of a bulb. It is all in how you are
Grounded. To bread I can see, I say, as it disappears and agrees
With me   the dark is drunk   and I am a man
Who turns on. I am a man.

"It is all in how you are grounded." Whether power and light
"only connect"; whether home is hell, or whether the dark is drunk;
whether I am a man who turns on; whether I am a man—"it is all
in how you are grounded!"

II. Parable and Picture

Which way *is left?* Maybe the passion and the pathos of the left,
which make us uncertain how to ask the question, can be suspended
long enough to keep the accent open. Maybe we could ask, without
the shouting evoked by dogmatism or despair, Which way *is left?*
To ask, Which way *is left?*—barely above a whisper—is to be
radically open to the way power and light "only connect." The
story of the ultimacy and urgency which bear down upon the fact
(from Nietzsche to Sartre, from Einstein to Norbert Wiener) is a
story of the ultimacy and urgency which bear down upon the fact
that "it *is* all in how you are grounded" with the force of an inclu-
sive judgment. Heaven and earth are involved in this judgment. All
peoples are caught up in it. Time is experienced as running out.
A sifting is taking place, separating the right from the left, judging
"between sheep and sheep, strengthening the weak and watching
over the fat and the strong." "All over hell the lights burn in your
eyes,/People are calling each other, weeping with a hundred thousand volts." Hell has inevitably, but nonetheless too suddenly, become history. "The fire that is ready for the devil and his angels" is
experienced as a consuming fire. Whether we are men who turn on,
indeed, whether we are men at all, depends in truth upon how we
are grounded. And how we are grounded is exposed by the finality

with which a liberating cause and a fulfilling commitment go together. Which way—*is*—*left?* Answer: *that* way, in *that* direction because *there* ultimacy and urgency, power and light, cause and commitment "only connect"—and a man turns on as a man!

"When the Son of Man comes in his glory and all the angels with him, he will sit in state on his throne, with all the nations gathered before him. He will separate men into two groups, as a shepherd separates the sheep from the goats, and he will place the sheep on his right hand and the goats on his left. Then the king will say to those on his right hand, 'You have my Father's blessing; come, enter and possess the kingdom that has been ready for you since the world was made. . . . I tell you this: anything you did for one of my brothers here, however humble, you did for me.' Then he will say to those on his left hand, 'The curse is upon you; go from my sight to the eternal fire that is ready for the devil and his angels. . . . I tell you this: anything that you did not do for one of these, however humble, you did not do for me.' "

We have here a combination of parable and picture. The picture is drawn by the author of the Gospel from the prophetic and apocalyptic imagery of final judgment. The parable is drawn from the precedent set by Ezekiel and placed by Matthew in the context of Jesus' familiar mode of teaching. But the parable carries the point and the power of the picture. There is an ultimacy and urgency by which the sheep are separated from the goats; and the test case is what was done or not done for "one of my brothers" —*anything,* for the brother, *however humble.*

A closer look at this "anything" narrows its range and zeroes in upon what it takes to turn a man on—as a man. "For when I was hungry, you gave me food; when thirsty, you gave me drink; when I was a stranger you took me into your home, when naked you clothed me; when I was ill you came to my help, when in prison you visited me." Hunger and thirst, clothing and shelter, loneliness overcome and bondage sprung—these are not only the basic needs of man in his concrete existence in nature and in history. They are also the fundamental prerequisites of the human meaning and fulfillment of his existence. Where these conditions are absent or denied, man driven by his need and the consequent search for them not only turns against his fellowman, but turns in upon himself. "To bread I can see, I say, as it disappears and agrees/With me, the dark is drunk, and I am a man who turns on." But to bread I cannot see, I shout:

> (fire stop thief murder save the world
>
> what world?
>   is it themselves these insects mean?
> when microscopic shriekings shall have snarled
> threads of celestial silence huger than
> eternity,men will be saviours
>   —flop
> grasshopper,exactly nothing's soon;
> scream,all ye screamers,till your if is up
> and vanish under prodigies of un)

Do you know why Mr. Cummings has put the shout within a parenthesis? I think it was because power and light, ultimacy and urgency, cause and commitment "only connect" when "how you are grounded" is experienced as your answer to a sovereign claim. The ultimate peril of the left is the disregard of this parenthesis. It contends, as does Sartre, that we live in a neutral world in which human freedom must create all meaning and value. "Men will be saviours!" But as yet no exit has been certified from ideological rivalries, bitter factionalisms, and utopian disillusionments—"intense prodigies of un," every one of them—which paralyze or dissipate the community of concern.

Our text, however, breaks quite new ground as regards the ethical sensitivity of the left. Concern for people in their basic needs and distresses finds wide recognition in Jewish piety and literature, as among the Buddhists, and along a broad front of humanistic humanitarianism, philosophical as well as political. But the picture and parable commended to us by Matthew make the quite unprecedented point: that Jesus is the Messiah, whose kingly claim and functions are chiefly expressed, not in the awesome transcendence of a majestic tribunal, but in the identification of himself with all sufferers in their humanity, and with all humanity in its sufferings. The consequence of this identification is that every social, cultural, institutional, valuational separation of men from one another has been set aside, and the least of the sons of men has become "brother" to the Son of Man.

There is only one radical and terrible separation, urgent because of its ultimacy, ultimate because no other connection between power and light, between a liberating cause and a fulfilling commitment, is finally possible and permanent. This is the separation between the sheep and the goats, the right and the left. Here the line is drawn at two subtle, self-revealing and self-judging points. The first marks the difference between a calculated and a spontaneous response to hunger and thirst, clothing and shelter, loneliness and bondage. The second marks the difference between self-justification and surprise. The goats are always ultimately certain that they have done what they could and are beyond question on the side of the Son of Man and his angels: "Lord, when was it that we saw you hungry or thirsty or a stranger or naked or ill or in prison, and did nothing for you?" The sheep, on the other hand, are ultimately surprised that they are not goats to be numbered with the devil and his angels: "Lord, when was it that we saw you hungry and fed you, or thirsty and gave you drink, a stranger and took you home, or naked and clothed you? When did we see you ill or in prison, and come to visit you?"

It may be that the commentators have been properly restrained in assuming an easy identification between the sheep and the right, the goats and the left. In doing so, however, they would seem to have blunted the ground-breaking force of the text itself. It is not enough to note the revolutionary force of the messianic humanism which affirms God's self-identification in the Christ with the intolerable sufferings of men. It is not enough—because it is *indeed* all in how you are grounded! Ultimacy and urgency do not connect if the finality of a liberating cause and a fulfilling commitment in Christ fail to include "one of my bothers here"—*NOW!* There is a further ground-breaking facet of the text which gives to its messianic humanism an unmistakably contemporary pertinence. This has to do with the geometric, if not with the apocalyptic, sense of the parable and the picture. The geometry identifies the sheep at the right hand of the king as being found of the king on the left hand of the world; and the same geometry identifies the goats at the left hand of the king as being found of the king on the right hand of the world! Thus it comes about that the left is not only on the side of the Son of Man and his angels; but the Son of Man and his angels are on the side of the left.

III. Possibility and Promise

Which way *is left?* When the passion and pathos of the new left are transformed by the parable and picture of the "messianic left," some glimpse of a perspective and a direction begins to emerge as an answer. Which way *is left?* The answer is: where ultimacy and urgency, power and light, a liberating cause and a fulfilling commitment "only connect"—and a man turns on as a man! Where they connect is where the basic needs and fundamental prerequisites of the humanity of man are lifted beyond self-justifying ideologies and power calculations to the level of spontaneity and surprise, and where justice has displaced enmity by reconciliation. On this level, the new left and the messianic left discover a marker which functions to keep them moving always toward one another and always ahead. "Here," says the marker, "is a way of possibility and promise." It is the way of possibility because it prevents the left from confusing the support of the Son of Man and his angels with its own achievements while continuing the struggle to achieve. It is the way of promise because it does not spare the left the pain of failure while holding before it the prospect of healing and renewal.

The uncanny messianic sensitivity and genius of Martin Luther put us in lively and concrete touch with this possibility and promise. In the course of a sermon which Luther once preached on this same text, he raised the question, Why did Christ give such singular emphasis to loving-kindness as the principal divide between the sheep and the goats? Luther's answer was that this was simply Christ's way of underlining how the fifth commandment was to be carried out.The fifth commandment, on Luther's reckoning, was "You shall not kill." Among other things, this means (as Luther explains in his Large Catechism) that every man is to be protected, liberated, from every other man's lust and violence, and thus the neighbor is to suffer no injury or harm.

Which way is left? Left is where the fifth commandment pinpoints the "only connect" between power and light—between ultimacy and urgency, between a liberating cause and a fulfilling commitment.

Well, here we are on the fifth Sunday in Lent. Tradition calls it *Dominica judica.* Vindication Sunday, the vindication being from deceitful and unjust men, according to Psalm 43:1. Once this was also the Sunday on which believers began with concentrated seriousness to face up to the crucifixion. It could be that not least among the claims giving direction to lives that have begun to be sensitive to the fifth commandment, is the liberating cause and fulfilling commitment of sharing with the new left the struggle to become the messianic left, so that a man may turn on as a man.

Meanwhile, "Friday's Child," as Mr. Auden calls his commemoration of Dietrich Bonhoeffer's martyrdom, is always before us and beside us:

> Now did He really break the seal
> And rise again? We dare not say;
> But conscious unbelievers feel
> Quite sure of Judgment Day.
>
> Meanwhile, a silence on the cross,
> As dead as we shall ever be,
> Speaks of some total gain or loss,
> And you and I are free
>
> To guess from the insulted face
> Just what appearances He saves
> By suffering in a public place
> A death reserved for slaves.

"When the Son of Man comes in his glory and all the angels with him . . . he will separate men into two groups, as a shepherd separates the sheep from the goats, and he will place the sheep on his right hand and the goats on his left."

A Time to Speak

Samuel Terrien

A time to keep silence, and a time to speak.

—*Eccles. 3:7*

Language belongs to the fabric of our faith. The Bible is "a scripture," but it was first and still remains a *Gesprochenheit,* "a spokenness." Deep may be calling wordlessly unto deep, but at the beginning was the Word. The gospel is "good news," and good news is announced by word of mouth as well as proclaimed by changed loves.

Yet, we labor in the midst of a crisis of language. As in Constantinople after the Fall of Rome, our speech is no longer trustworthy. It is devalued. The credibility gap begins with any first utterance. Is this, then, "a time to speak" or "a time to keep silence"?

I

Language betrays us because we have abused it, especially in the church, where too many assertions have been, in effect, little more than exercises in double-talk destined not to offend either the pious or the impious. Thus, the pulpit has often ignored intellectual integrity in matters of biblical criticism, because a scientific approach to Scripture might upset the serenity of Sunday school memories. Or again it has dulled the horror of the cross or studiously avoided talking about the fear of God because such themes repel modern minds and must be considered obsolete.

As a result of these two contradictory illusions, religious language has become strangely clean, antiseptic, and meaningless. The particularity of Christian faith is diluted into religiosity. One still talks about it because it is probably a good basis for an ethics of goodwill toward all men. Has not *ecumenical* become a synonym for *tolerant?*

We no longer know how to speak the truth, because we have lost the ability to speak the truth of love. The crisis of religious language reveals the crisis of our faith. It is because our faith is weak that we are no longer articulate. We reenter the Paleolithic Age of the grunt, for we are the magicians of the Technological Age, we take the proximate for the ultimate, and we are embarrassed by the holy.

No wonder that a large part of contemporary philosophy reflects the movement of "linguistic analysis." To examine the meaning of words and the structure of speech would not be a bad thing, if only it did not become an end in itself instead of remaining a tool for asking the final questions of existence: What is man? What is life? What is it to be? Where are we going?

In the meantime, incomprehension divides men over the face of the planet. And this is not just the failure of speaking a common tongue, like Esperanto. In plain English:

> . . . Words strain,
> Crack and sometimes break, under the burden,
> Under the tension, slip, slide, perish,
> Decay with imprecision, will not stay in place,
> Will not stay still. . . .

Shall we then resort to silence?

II

Silence has much in its favor. There are many forms of language which do not need words. "Day unto day uttereth speech," and "their voice is not heard, yet their chant goeth out through all the earth."

The natural scientist perceives and interprets the signs which appear in the universe. The speechless language of science permits us today to distinguish once again between a finite cosmos and the ultimate reality. Scientific language is essentially nonverbal, for it proceeds from mathematical measurement.

The painter also understands the wordless language of the dialogue between nature and man. The artist discovers a dimension of truth which is concealed from the average eye, and he prepares us to open up the depths of our being to that truth. This is not achieved, however, without agonies, deaths of the self, and resurrections. "Art is a likeness of creation," wrote Paul Klee in his notebooks. "The heart that beats in this world seems mortally wounded in me." Even in its seemingly most secular, the authentic art of today sees the Spirit of God, dovelike, hovering "over the vast abyss," and bringing at a cost life out of chaos.

Music is par excellence the speechless language of man's encounter with infinity. Not necessarily church music, incidentally, but rather those abstract pieces, like the final bars of Beethoven's last piano sonata, modulating man's reach for the beyond. Asked Igor Stravinsky, "To what shall I cling in order to escape the dizziness that seizes me before the virtuality of this infinitude?"

The poet, of course, uses words, but his language assumes in fact a supraverbal quality. Through a spell-like short-circuiting of the intellectual processes, he is able "to contact the immensities" and thus to produce "instantaneous conviction."

Shall we then conclude that religious language is no longer desirable or even possible? Are we not in the desperate need to be reticent about God?

III

A case may surely be made against the use of words in the context of faith. One may even ask whether human speech is ever appropriate either in religion or in love. I know a happily married couple who have debated humorously for thirty years on the merit and danger of talking about romantic love. Does one deepen or weaken the passion of love by making it verbally explicit?

The prophet Elijah on Mount Horeb recognized the presence of the Lord only when he heard "the sound of utter silence"—not the "still small voice" of moral conscience, as we usually say. And the apostle Paul refused to analyze or even to translate into words the memory of his ineffable ecstasy. "Whether in the body or without," he knew not.

Even someone who belongs to a Latin culture, where the use of words is far from discouraged, may be permitted to shrink from Anglo-Saxon, Protestant subjectivism, which urges testimony about one's own "religious experience," that fetish of our time. Nothing is more immodest than religious immodesty. Fortunately, it was a Scot, James Moffatt, who was able to joke at this form of obscenity. When asked at a prayer meeting, "Have you found Jesus?" He replied, "No! Is he lost?" I am inclined to stay away from spiritual retreats which turn into talkfests. For years I have seriously suggested that such events should take place in zoological gardens. One might do worse, as a starter for spiritual recollection, than looking silently at penguins and other jailed creatures of our world!

The vision of the holy is far too traumatic for words. The prophet Isaiah could only say, "Woe is me, I am undone!" When the Lord spoke to Job from the whirlwind, he had no taste for rhetoric. Silence is the language of adoration.

Should religion, therefore, be speechless? Not in the least. There is "a time to keep silence," and there is "a time to speak."

IV

When the Verrazano Bridge was built over the narrows in the New York Lower Bay, one could watch, twenty-four hours a day, with gigantic floodlights during the night, the immense cables that would have been too heavy for ordinary manufacture and transportation. Enormous wheels would twist and twist hundreds of strands of thin wire across the water into the darkness or the fog, and little by little the huge cables would thicken to their proper strength.

This is the speechless symbol of the power and the nature of our faith: an active waiting in hope, as the semantic image of the Hebrew word for hope, *tiqwah,* suggests, while the rope is being woven for flexibility and resistance in a world of constant tension. Faith creates the power to support in order to carry. Thus, it should never be confused with individual experiences of ecstasy, or even a feeling of presence. On the contrary, it is when God is absent that we are called to have faith: the response of man to the memory and the anticipation of the presence of the Holy God in the life of the church through the centuries.

It is faith which permits us to repeat with the old patriarch, "How awesome is this place: surely the Lord is here! This is none other than the house of God, and this is the gate of heaven." It is faith which makes us resident aliens in the Temple, bystanders at the cross, and members of that handful of disciples, scattered after the fiasco of their loyalty, but rallied and pardoned, as the Christ commissions us with them and says, "Lo, I shall be with you alway, even unto the end of the world!"

Faith is not a felt experience. Rather it is a discipline of daily athletics of the spirit, manifesting itself supremely by taking part in the Lord's Supper. There, the Word is acted out, but it is not voiceless, for the sermon must always accompany the celebration of the Eucharist, just as the sermon remains idle talk unless it stems from, and leads to, the mystery of Holy Communion, and thus may become the Sacrament of the Word.

Language must sooner or later be used to express the stirrings from the deep. Human words become then the bearers of the holy, not when they display the preacher's smartness or even piety, but when they exhibit objectively the intervention of God in the Israel of the human race—that invisible church of all those who wait for a better world and work at it.

Some churches of high liturgical tradition practice what is called "the monstrance of the host." In Reformed Christendom, genuine preaching is the monstrance of the gospel. The language of the Word may change and will change in the bewildering world of tomorrow, but it will not be the language of the world. For there is a story to be told. God so loved the world that he gave his only Son. God is not an idea. He is a person who enters our humanity, bears the burden of our guilt, and heals our wounds.

This is the reason for which faith knows the difference between good and evil, even when it is compelled to choose a lesser evil. Faith affirms the triumph of life over death. Faith knows that love is power. Faith discerns that there is a quality of humaneness which transcends the peculiarity of race, of tongue, of national allegiance. Faith has the courage to say that choices have to be made, and decisions taken. There is a time to speak.

Let us pray: O God, quicken us to the true, to the beautiful, and to the good, and open our lips that thy word may not return to thee void.

In the name of the Word made flesh,
Even Jesus Christ our Lord, *Amen.*

Creatures of a Creator, Members of a Body, Subjects of a Kingdom

George H. Williams

> *Do not be conformed to this world but be*
> *transformed by the renewal of your mind,*
> *that you may prove what is the will of God,*
> *what is good and acceptable and perfect.*
>
> *—Rom. 12:2 (RSV)*

I wish to reflect on the implications of our Christian affirmation that we are creatures of the Creator; that we are severally members of a mystical Body, for the church includes the blessed dead which are in the Lord, and the yet unborn; and finally that we are subjects of a kingdom yet to be.

Some of you may feel ill at ease with these metaphors of spiritual subordination. Some of you might say, recoiling from the suggestion of submissiveness, "To be sure, our Scripture and tradition are indeed full of regal references and speak much about the coming of the kingdom, but we are not free citizens, indeed sovereign citizens; and does not the perpetuation of older political metaphors tend to inhibit Christian social action and sanction acquiescence in the status quo?"

It is my conviction, as a church historian, that in the realm of grace we are in fact subjects, not sovereign citizens. This is one of the mysteries of the kingdom. Matthew and Luke preserve warnings about the difficulty of identifying either the kingdom or the Messiah. False prophets of the kingdom will come and show signs, "that they may lead astray, if possible, the elect." In the realm of grace one is chosen, one is enrolled among the elect, one is prepared to offer ultimate obedience to a Sovereign above and beyond the kingdoms of this world.

Likewise is it with membership in the Body. The metaphor of *member* is often lost on us. Romans 12:1–8 reminds us of its specificities. The Head of the Body is Christ. Although the body metaphor has admittedly often functioned to consolidate social conservatism in both the body politic and the Body ecclesiastical, each with its classes or hierarchy, nevertheless the metaphor could always be corrected on this score through that great equalizing text of I Corinthians 2:15–16: "The spiritual man judges all things. . . . for we, severally, have the mind of Christ." The Body of Christ, as it were, becomes temporarily visible in Holy Communion. And as grace and obedience are the marks of anticipation of the kingdom, so love and mutual aid are the marks of the oneness in the Body. There is a parallel to Paul's body metaphor of Romans 12 in I Corinthians 12. This more extended version is, you recall, followed by the famous paean to love in chapter 13: "Love bears all things." This love within the Body and extending to *all* creatures (even beyond that Body) was felt by Paul to be so distinctive that he eschewed the Greek word *eros,* susceptible though it was of the most noble connotations, and used instead *agape.* For *agape* has compassion even for what may be unlovely, for what may appear to lack worth.

Likewise radical in its implications is our sense of creatureliness and ultimate dependence. Our fellow creatures, the plants and the animals, know not, of course, that they are creatures. And even among our fellowmen a creature-consciousness is not widespread. Paul observed that "ever since the creation of the world his [God's] invisible nature . . . has been clearly perceived in the things that have been made." And Paul went on to insist that atheists were "without excuse; for although they knew God [as Creator], they did not honor him as God or give thanks to him . . . and their senseless minds were darkened." Paul presupposed an aboriginal monotheism from which mankind had fallen away. We today, of course, have a different perspective, and understand that the religious apprehension of utter dependence upon the creative power bringing the world into being from primordial chaos, represents in fact an advanced stage in the evolution of the consciousness of mankind. But Paul's acerb judgment about the small proportion of the race who descry the Creator in perceiving that we are creatures remains valid.

As grace and obedience mark the subject of the kingdom, and

as love and compassion should betoken membership in the Body of Christ, so creature-consciousness is marked, not by groveling self-abasement, but by that solemn joy which finds expression either in reverent restraint or in exultant praise.

Yet there is probably not a one of us here who has not at some time wondered whether there be after all such a realm. And surely many people outside the church, more incredulous than hostile, more indifferent than indulgent, would simply remark, "We behold no Creator; we see no Body but what you yourself know is bread, and as for a Body ecclesiastical, it is dismembered, and by your divisions you belie the One Holy Catholic Church which you credally proclaim; and as for your kingdom, you Christians have chronically confused it with empire, church, nation, and even class or race. Besides, when it comes to order, love, and what you call grace, we who are without the church think that we experience whatever little of these there is in life in about the same degree as you do, perhaps even better, for not becoming involved in organized religion and its endemic rancors. Even your Jesus seems to have been very much an individualist, out among the lilies of the field; a nonconformist, consorting with publicans and prostitutes."

And in answer we would acknowledge that all these observations have considerable validity. The prophets, the evangelists, and the apostles to whom we listen in this place regularly remind us of the same. Yet it is here in the sanctuary also, in our readings and anthems, that we acknowledge that we are creatures. It is in our praise and prayer that we testify to an impending realm of grace. It is in our ordinances or sacraments that we show forth how we are reborn in grace and how, though ever alone, we are one Body in memory and hope.

As the author of the second-century Epistle to Diognetus said, although we Christians live in diverse places, "as each man's lot has been cast, and follow the customs of the country in clothing and food . . . at the same time . . . [we, hopefully] give proof of the remarkable and admittedly extraordinary constitution of . . . [our] own commonwealth." We behave as creatures before an invisible Creator; we are moved with compassion for fellow creatures whom we consider members of the same Body, or potentially—all mankind; and we count ourselves subjects, perhaps kneeling or bowing in prayer, of a wholly invisible Sovereign. The constitution of our commonwealth, the church, is indeed remarkable, and our behavior within its precincts and beyond admittedly extraordinary; but most of the time we know why we act this way, in faith, and sometimes we are even encouraged by the thought, to quote again the ancient correspondent of Diognetus, that this kind of fealty helps hold together not only ourselves but, in the long sweeps of history, also society and even the world. In the various transactions in the sanctuary, we speak or pray or praise out of compassion for the whole world. In the concentric circles of our awareness we may, to be sure, begin with our own problematic self, but we move outward from the immediate circle of kinship to the ever larger circles of the local community, to the nation and our particular community of nations, to humanity in time and space. The church is the self-conscious bearer and steward of the memory and the hope of an ideal mankind, summed up in our faith in Jesus Christ as the Second and the Last Adam.

As we, from the sanctuary, look out upon the world, it is important to observe that, in nearly two thousand years of Christian history, we have collectively purified and clarified our understanding of what biblical Hebrews and the early Christians called somewhat disparagingly the world or the Gentiles without the law or the gospel. We may observe three successive attitudes toward the world. Early Christians, including most of the New Testament writers, were *censorious.* After the establishment of Christianity by Constantine, Christians became increasingly *coercive,* imposing the regnant view (as Orthodox and Catholic) on each other and on nonbelievers, sometimes even by Inquisition and religious war. At long last, Christianity, whether churchly and ecumenical or sectarian and inward-turning, has largely come to eschew the older modalities of censure and coercion, and come to nurture instead a nonjudgmental compassion: that is, a fellow feeling for the vagaries of the common human condition.

But a sensitized conscience and an expanded compassion often lead to identification with the world beyond the church and even, imperceptibly, to conformity with the world. Many liberals in our midst, for instance, including those in the latent church and those in the residual church, find it charmingly plausible in *Jesus Christ Superstar* that he who once protected the woman taken in adultery from stoning is portrayed as not only the redeemer of Mary Magdalene but also her favorite lover as well. We must again be reminded of the salt that loses its savor and of the leaven which, though its function is to permeate the lump, does so only because of its special character and concentration of essence.

I have been talking about the church as made up of Christians in the modalities of creature, member, and subject because, as we think in the sanctuary about the problems that beset us as Christians and as citizens, it is not always clear, either to ourselves or to others, whom we are addressing when we consider such matters as civil rights and black empowerment, war in Indochina, sexual behavior, divorce, abortion, drugs, etc. These problems are not only around us but also among us as Christians; and it is not always clear whether, in our compassion, we are clarifying what we deem proper for Christians, or for society at large; or, again, whether we are thinking of personal behavior in the private domain, or of laws and other restraints or inducements in the public domain.

Consider, now, just one of these public-private, moral-religious, societal-Christian problems. It is an issue in which this congregation is probably not divided down the middle but rather is ranged pretty much on what you would consider the liberal and compassionate side. Indeed, almost all Protestant denominations in Canada and the United States have by now officially spoken on this same side. I refer, of course, to abortion. I appear in this distinguished pulpit at the special bidding of the Preacher to the University in order that the minority conviction among Protestants on this issue might be given resonance in this place. And I wish to make my point as it might commend itself to members of the Body of Christ, to would-be subjects of the kingdom, to those who acknowledge that we are but creatures, that is, to you as practicing Christians, and secondarily to you as citizens of the Commonwealth, with implications for public domain.

There is no text in the New Testament directed specifically against abortion. But our beautiful passage from the Epistle to

Diognetus is representative of all patristic literature at this point when it declares, Christians "beget children, but they do not cast out their offspring." This statement refers primarily to the exposure of unwanted children, or to their sale into slavery by poverty-pressed parents. There are many other patristic texts expressly directed against abortion, and at every stage. Indeed, Christian abhorrence of such an act was, in the eyes of pagans, one of the marks of early Christianity. A modern authority on the subject has rightly called opposition to the taking of life in the womb an almost absolute value in Christian history until most recent times.

Many scriptural passages came to be woven into the Christian view of the sacredness of intrauterine life: instruction as to the might of the mustard seed, wonder at God's shaping each one in the womb (Job 31:15; Isa. 44:24, etc.), praise for God's exaltation of those of low degree, fear of offense against the least and the little ones, fascination that the baby John, destined to be the Baptist, leapt for joy in the womb of his mother, Elizabeth, at the approach and salutation of the Virgin Mary.

In the Old Testament there is one text that deals with abortion, though obliquely—Exodus 21:22: "When men strive together, and hurt a woman with child, so that there is a miscarriage, . . . the one who hurt her shall be fined." When this sole and incidental passage came to be translated into the Greek Septuagint, at a time when Hellenistic Jews had come to share with Greek philosophers a sensitized concern for all intrauterine life, they altered the foregoing verse so that it quite specifically distinguished between a second-degree and a first-degree abortion, amplifying it thus: "If . . . her child comes forth while it is not yet formed, then the penalty shall be a money payment . . . ; but if it was formed, then he [the man responsible in the tussle] shalt give his life for that life." This augmented Septuagintal version of Exodus 21:22 passed into the legal usage of Greek and Latin Christendom as, on this point, authoritative over the Hebrew version, although the gravity of the penalty was considerably mitigated. This Hellenistic Jewish interpretation of the passage continued to shape the canon law, the common law, and then the statutory law of all Christendom, including the laws in our American states. As the soul, anciently, was thought to give form to the inchoate being within the womb, formation by the rational soul, or animation or quickening, was in antiquity and in the Middle Ages considered the decisive moment after which abortion, always considered by Christians as sinful, became a crime. The embryological theory behind all this was, of course, as rudimentary as the theological. It presupposed that the male seed was preeminent, drawing only nutriment from the matrix. Indeed this sire-centered theory of genetics explains in part why the Catholic Church continued for so long virtually to equate, in moral gravity, contraception and abortion. But in 1827 a German biologist proved that the new life in the womb results from the union of the sperm and the equally influential ovum, and much later in that century chromosomes were identified and their number in sperm and ovum observed to be half of those in the zygote. In the meantime papal teaching, moving beyond Aristotle and Thomas Aquinas by way of the Septuagintal version of Exodus 21:22 with its distinction between an unformed and a formed fetus, brought the Catholic position on abortion abreast of the new genetic and fetological facts and included the concept itself under the plenary protection of the church's prohibition of abortion.

The absoluteness of the papal position on the right of the fetus was admittedly established at the expense of the mother in the rare case of tragic dilemma; and almost all Protestants recoiled from such absolutism. Furthermore, Protestants, with their married clergy, were earlier sensitive to women's rights and, under the influence of the social gospel, became concerned with the conditions of children and their families in poverty and exploitation. Then, most recently, the conjunction of the global population crisis, the ecological deterioration, the sexual revolution, and the second great phase of the women's rights movement has conspired to turn the attention of most Protestants to other pressing issues and to obscure, as I would maintain, the still valid Christian heritage. And an intra-Christian schism of conscience has developed on the issue. It has thus been left primarily to the Catholic Church to defend what I consider not merely Christian but the essentially humane cause. Liberal Protestants, long identified in America with defending the rights of the downtrodden and of all those whose cries are not heard in the councils of the mighty, have on this issue heeded, it would seem, only the voice of sovereign womanhood, while turning a deaf ear to the cries for succor from within the womb.

Surely the mother is sovereign over her own body, but no more than cosovereign with society at large over any new life gestating within her. In the realm of the kingdom we know that the presence of a Sovereign in our lives is most palpable in the experience of grace or mercy. Surely we are creatures; and no less than lemmings we must control our numbers or eventually leap into the abyss of world chaos and famine. But, as never before, with creaturely restraint and reverence before the mystery of creation we should hold back from doing certain things now technically within our power, whether it be disturbing the Van Allen Belt, filling in the coastal wetlands, or manipulating life from conception to senility.

The abomination of desolation in Daniel (9:27, etc.) and in the Synoptic Apocalypse (Matt. 24:15; Mark 13:14) was the emplacement of the man of sin, some idol (cf. II Thess. 2:1–12), in the completely empty sanctuary of the Temple in Jerusalem, which emptiness had symbolized for Jews and early Christians alike the presence of the Invisible Creator of heaven and earth. Hitler and Himmler, who set out eugenically to propagate the superman and who established the norms for the elimination of all forms of "unworthwhile life," should be sufficient warning that in an age of technological and manipulative power of frightening potential, the intrusion of the man of sin (that is, omnicompetent, know-it-all man) in the place of the Creator can be vastly more ominous in its consequences than in the time of Herod's Temple and the impostures of the Emperor Caligula. For Christians, the body is the temple of the Creator-Spirit: and in a special sense is this true of the body of a mother. In that mysterious maternal darkness whence we all precariously emerge, let there be no abomination of desolation!—be it the eugenicizing state, be it the presumption of absolute sexual autonomy. As Christians, members of one Body in time and space, surely we must evolve ever new modalities of compassion and mutual aid, and that means for women and girls with unwanted pregnancies. But surely also a sense of mystery before the Word of God, conceived of the Holy Ghost in Mary great with child, must restrain us as Christians from any facile acceptance of the view that every mother is absolute sovereign over the body within her own.

Many Protestants, who presumably would not themselves resort to abortion, would nevertheless argue that abortion is a private and not a public matter, and that any kind of coercion here is improper in the public domain. But here they confuse sexual freedom with something of a quite different order. One need not, to counter their allegedly tolerant view, adduce a parallel with murder. The reason that abortion has never been, even in the most extreme legal and canonical formulations, equated with murder is that the fetus is indeed, in a sense, a creature of its parents. Thus where the mother has not even by what might be called the consent of passion acceded to the possibility of conception, as for example in rape, present laws and medical practice countenance the vindication of the victim of sexual violence, leaving it to her soveriegn mercy to decide whether to proceed with the pregnancy. I refrain in this setting from going into other exceptions or the theory thereof, to get to my main point, which is my civil-libertarian concern for the most defenseless entities in the body politic.

Most of us rejoice in the constitutional or de facto recession everywhere of capital punishment. Even the notorious Manson family has now won the right to life, because a growing sensibility all over the Western world has come to recoil from any corporate taking of life, even of the most craven criminal. But sensitive as we have become to prisoners within the walls of penitentiaries, many are, I think, strangely indifferent to the innocent and expectant denizens within the supposedly protective walls of their mothers' bodies. People today, so much better informed about embryology than their forebears, who could but grope for what constituted the beginnings of life, still facilely speak of that mere "blob" or "tissue," even though they need only turn their eyes to those amazing color photographs that show the fetus a strong swimmer in the amniotic fluid, susceptible to pain and elementary gratifications long before the mother herself is even aware of what an older embryology called quickening or ensoulment.

I cannot help feeling that, just as the otherwise farseeing fathers of our republic who declared that all men are created free and equal could nevertheless be blind to the black man (reckoned as but three-fifths of a person and even then solely for computing white representation in the Congress), so broad-minded people today, concerned with social justice, and color-blind at last, are, however, as it were, night-blind. Just because the little limbs and head that are surgically snipped or the little body that is salted out is in the darkness of another body claiming sole sovereignty over it, many people see no evil. Nor is microscopic abortion morally less grave for being less palpably bloody.

I hold that the state most assuredly does have responsibility for the protection of human life wherever it is, as also for the prevention of cruelty, be that in respect to the fetus in the womb, or to the battered child in the home, or to the mistreated animal in the street or in the laboratory; be it the senile, the almost nameless, and the forgotten in the nursing home and the asylum. As the life of any of these is withdrawn from the protection of the body politic, in that measure are we all diminished and our lives rendered more precarious and subdued for ever more arbitrary manipulation.

The ancient Roman paterfamilias had the right of life and death over the fetus within the womb of his wife; and not only could he sell his own child into slavery as its sire, but he could even in some circumstances lawfully put a son to death. To this day, according to Afghan law, it is the father who actually steps forward to execute the capital punishment decreed by the Muslim state, since the father is deemed the primary sovereign over his son whatever the age. Western civilization will have made no advance on this score if, in the present climate of sexual permissiveness amid ecological crisis, we accord now to the woman a prerogative that in the evolution of Western civilization was finally wrested from the omnipotent male.

We simply cannot with moral impunity reduce the whole transaction of life or death in the womb to the level of privatized morality. We cannot consent to its trivialization as a merely medical incident involving only a prospective mother and her physician or social worker. The zygote with its redoubled chromosomes, its genetic code set, needs only time to become one of us.

Without self-discipline in the intimacies of our sexuality, without acknowledgment that our loving companionship rides ultimately upon the great river of life which is our potentially creative sexuality, then that mysterious channel may eventually overflow into a casual network of run-off ditches, there to stagnate or to become even bitter as brine in the dead sea of sexual self-absorption; and then the great current of joy, fecundity, and companionableness ordained by our Creator may no longer flow naturally to refresh and irrigate the plains of ordinary life.

We are creatures, we are subjects, we are members of a Body. As creatures, may we know the bounds of our habitation, and as stewards of creation become more concerned for all our fellow creatures. As subjects of One who has shown us the Way of life and the Way of death, may we not be submissive to what passes for the wisdom and prudence of the world. As members of the Body of Christ, may we extend our compassion and mutual aid toward all within the body ecclesiastical and also the body politic.

With a sense of purpose in the evolutionary and historical
                  unfolding of life,
With a sense of meaningfully belonging to a Body that
                  comprehends the generations,
    that is, all the saints who from their labors rest
                  and the unborn,
With a sense for the sustaining order of the universe
                  amid the vast
    precariousness and random of all that goes on within
                  both sidereal and submolecular
                  space,

Let us pray:

O thou in whose fingers are the spaces and the times,
Bless and uphold us,
As we in our period, formations of togetherness in thy name,
    Emit the signals of our creaturely praise.
                  In Jesus' name, *Amen.*

Christ's Liberating Mandate

Merrill R. Abbey

And as he was setting out on his journey, a man ran up and knelt before him, and asked him, "Good Teacher, what must I do to inherit eternal life?"

—*Mark 10:17 (RSV)*

One sentence in the tenth chapter of Mark sets up the kind of tension within us that magnetizes attention. "You lack one thing," we hear Jesus saying; "go, sell what you have, and give to the poor, and you will have treasure in heaven; and come, follow me." This cuts across the grain of our self-interest. It so contradicts our social philosophy and economic assumptions that we are hard pressed to understand. We need to approach it with more than usual prayerfulness.

A hard saying, but not harsh. Jesus, the Gospel notes, looking at his questioner, loved him. His honest, urgent query evoked an answer meant to help. "Good Teacher," the man asked, "what must I do to inherit eternal life?" His search was not primarily for endless existence; he sought life fulfilled. How could he live with durable purpose? What could free him from his round of meaningless pursuits? How could he rise above frustration? "More powerful frustration is the lot of the more powerful," Aly Wassil observed. Not knowing why, this man of power was filled with frustration.

Arthur Miller's play *The Price* reflects his hunger. Solomon, an aged furniture dealer, has spent his adult years trying to put substantial, worthy furniture in the hands of buyers. The flimsy stuff filling the market saddens him. It seems to him symptomatic of our life. We are uncomfortable as we gather around a strong, solid table, he reflects. Under our hand it feels as if it would last a lifetime. Looking at the relationships of the family gathered around it, we wonder if they will so endure. Is the table more substantial than the life we are making? So he continues, "What is the key word today? Disposable. The more you can throw it away the more it is beautiful. The car, the furniture, the wife, the children —everything has to be disposable." From this sad plight the man seeking eternal life wanted liberation. He was asking: How can I find a quality of life liberated from the tyranny of the disposable?

Two brothers are central to the play—one a wealthy, widely recognized surgeon, the other a moderately secure but unhappy policeman. In a long-cherished dream, the policeman and his wife have planned to break with their routine existence, return to school, complete college degrees, and enter work that they hope may promise more of challenge and growth. The bondage of security and the dependable paycheck has immobilized them. Looking back over the years, the wife sees a sad meaning: "Everything was always temporary with us. It's like we never were anything, we were always about-to-be."

That too entered into the need of the man asking the way to eternal life. He knew the need not only for purpose and meaning to outlast the "disposable," but for power to *be* in some authentic way, freed from the limbo of "always about-to-be."

Jesus, looking at him, loved him, and told him: What you seek is a gift God offers. You cannot earn it. Much less can you win it by conquest. You can only receive and accept it. Yet some things stand in its way. From them you need liberation. "Go, sell what you have, and give to the poor, and you will have treasure in heaven; and come, follow me."

Does our sense of shock at these words come from the fact that, with this man, we ask a religious question and receive an answer which plunges us into the affairs of the world? The quest for eternal life implies things done before an altar; the answer sends us into the marketplace of owning, buying, selling, giving. Wanting eternal life—which is life with God—the man addressed Jesus as "Good Teacher." "Why do you call me good?" Jesus replied, "No one is good but God alone." What such a questioner seeks does not belong to any teacher to give. No manipulation can produce it. Only God can give it.

As if to underscore this religious dimension of the quest, Jesus added, "Keep the commandments." When the seeker declared that he had done all this and was still dissatisfied, Jesus offered his liberating mandate: "One thing you lack; go, sell . . . give . . . come, follow me." The answer had moved from the altar to the world outside.

Such memorable leaders as William Temple and Francis J. McConnell noted that, of all world faiths, the Christian faith is the most materialistic. Its revelation of God comes enfleshed: "The Word became flesh and dwelt among us." God, eternal, omnipotent, all-holy, entered our life as a baby cradled in a manger, went about among us as a carpenter, died on a cross, was buried in a tomb, and came forth to meet with fishermen in the outlands of Galilee. Other religions talk of the immortality of the soul; Christians affirm, "I believe in the resurrection of the body." Although the declaration does not mean resuscitation of the flesh, it does look to the renewal of a total life in which you continue to be you— recognizably you. Paul visualized the resurrected life as that of a "spiritual" body, but he was too much a realist to dream of life without some bodily instrument.

One of Christianity's earliest tests plunged it into a struggle with Gnostic teachers who thought of Jesus as less than fully human. The Christian way, they taught, hung on esoteric spiritual secrets, not on conduct toward other people in down-to-earth relationships and bread-and-butter issues. The New Testament would have nothing of such disembodied spirituality; many of its documents were written to refute the notion. Jesus depicted final judgment as a verdict on our response to those who are hungry, thirsty, strangers, without clothes, sick, or in prison. Such is the materialism of our faith.

Pope Paul VI shows a reason. The gospel insists that every child of God has a right to *be* something. But in order to be something, a man must *know* something and *have* something. We need a floor under our feet. There is a level of food, health, housing, and education below which a man cannot be allowed to sink and still achieve full humanity. Identifying himself with men's needs in these matters, Jesus gave support to the full humanity of "the least of these," to which the meeting of basic creature wants is prerequisite.

Philosopher of instant communication Marshall McLuhan has taught us to think of ourselves as inhabitants of a global village. Let us think of the village for a moment. Picture the world shrunk to a village of a thousand, keeping present ratios of distribution of wealth and income intact. Nearly half the people of such a village, 495 of the thousand, would be eking out a dying existence on less than $100 per person per year. Roughly two-thirds, 670 of the thousand, would be living on $300 a year. Only about one in nine, some 115 persons, would have as much as $1,000 a year. That puts all of us in the tiny, select group of the world's wealthy—and lends terrifying force to Jesus' saying about "the least of these."

When we fail them, full life escapes both them and us. We can see that in terms of potential sickness and health. Food experts say there are now more *hunger-weakened* people in the world than there were *people* in 1875. That is a vast arsenal of explosive potential for the spark of a virus out of control. Or we can see it in terms of world disorder. When he was secretary of defense, Robert McNamara cited figures to support his contention that the world's hunger map coincides with the map of violent disorder. The areas of deepest poverty generate the most intense violence. Or we can see it in terms of the breakdown of trust within our own domestic life. While we devoted major stores of wealth to warfare in a peasant nation, our life at home was haunted by a troubled conscience and a shattering of the unities that could restore creative purpose among us.

These are crass ways of stating an inescapable truth. Some major sharing with the needs of the sick, hungry, impoverished peoples of the world is essential to our entrance into the fulfilled life we want for ourselves and our children. We need Christ's liberating mandate if we are to live to the full.

Is this too forbidding? Is our Lord's demand impossible? How can we separate ourselves from the things we have? Our quandary is written into the Gospel incident. The man who asked eternal life "went away sorrowful; for he had great possessions." Ruefully, Jesus observed, "It is easier for a camel to go through the eye of a needle than for a rich man to enter the kingdom of God." What could he have meant by this extravagant saying?

It is one with the steady New Testament insistence that we do not earn the life of the kingdom of God; we can only receive and accept it. To know our weakness and need is to be heirs of the kingdom: "Blessed are the poor in spirit, for theirs is the kingdom of God." The life of the kingdom is characterized not so much by the wielders of power as by its victims: "Blessed are those who are persecuted for righteousness' sake, for theirs is the kingdom of heaven." Not as self-sufficient, achieving what we need, do we come to God, but as children who must receive treasure and sustenance as gifts from those on whom they utterly depend: "Whoever does not receive the kingdom of God like a child shall not enter it." Yet what we own or have achieved gets such a hold upon us that entering into fulfilled life as dependent suppliants seems all but unthinkable.

The grip of our technology is an instance. Our ability to do a thing becomes almost a compulsion to do it. One of the leading physicists who developed the atomic bomb gives a case in point. "We made it," he said, "in order to prevent it being used . . . by Hitler. In the end it turned out that there wasn't any German atomic bomb project. . . . But then we used it all the same." In our present environmental crisis we are discovering that the existence of the means of doing a thing is almost a guarantee that we will do it, no matter what the threat to ecological balance and our own future. For good or ill, the means we own control us.

It is so even of intangibles we all value. The man who sought eternal life was rich in such intangibles—moral rectitude, religious aspiration, the wit to put a timeless question to the greatest Teacher. With a simple honesty which Jesus accepted, he could say of the commandments, "All these I have observed from my youth." Yet frustration chained him. Moral rightness can make us censorious and judgmental toward others, tense and brittle within ourselves. Being consciously right does not assure personal fulfillment.

Slowly we learn how true this is of our coveted academic and professional intangibles. In the play we have quoted, the surgeon brother has climbed to the top of his profession. His contributions to medical science have been acclaimed. He is one of the recognized great in his field. Have his losses been part of the price? He is estranged from his brother, divorced from his wife, alienated from his children. Looking back, he reflects, "You start out wanting to be the best, and there's no question that you do need a certain fanaticism; there's so much to know and so little time. Until you've eliminated everything extraneous—including people. And of course the time comes when you realize you haven't been specializing in something—something has been specializing in you. You become a kind of instrument, an instrument that cuts money out of people, or fame out of the world." Possessed by good things he thought he owned, he needed Christ's liberating mandate. Does he hold a mirror for some of us?

One thing changes this from bad news to good. There is a grace that can break the grip of the good things that own us. Shocked as we are, the disciples asked, "Then who can be saved?" "With men it is impossible," Jesus replied, "but not with God; for all things are possible with God." His love can reach us and make us loving. His goodness can win our trust and help us to live by faith, not sight. This grace can free us from things which started as means and became tyrannical ends we pursued by compulsion.

I have recently met two men who seemed to have found this freedom. One, an eye surgeon, clearly showed in his life a quality which his professional success could not explain. Several months of each year he moves his practice to one of the world's deep poverty areas, bringing healing and sight to people who cannot pay for his services. In serving those who otherwise would be unserved he has found an obvious fulfillment.

The other man, a contractor, responded to the need of his parish-supported medical missionary for a new hospital. With his skill as a builder he went to Nicaragua and constructed it. He had, first, to teach local workmen how to make concrete blocks and how to use the new building materials and methods. He had to train and equip workmen who built roads into the remote area, over which building supplies could be brought in. In so doing, he not only built a needed hospital, he revitalized the economy and social organization of the region. He also enlarged his own world and, by the grace of God, found unexpected realization of things not disposable but enduringly fulfilling.

St. Augustine spoke of how, before his son's birth, nobody wanted him. Yet after he came, they could not help loving him; so they called him Adeodatus, "God-given." Isn't it so with our Lord? He comes with a mandate too stern to accept. Yet when we receive him this mandate becomes liberating. We find in him the Friend without whom we could not live half so fully, and he becomes to us Adeodatus, "God-given."

Resisting and Welcoming the New

Walter Harrelson

Ephraim's iniquity is bundled up, his sin stored up; birth pangs come upon him, but he is an unwise son. At his time he won't stand at the breach made for sons to be born.

—Hosea 13:12–13

This text from the prophet Hosea lays out the problem of human life in its tragic and exciting possibilities. New life awaits us but, in the grip of birth pangs, men refuse to cooperate in being born.

The image of death and rebirth is one of the oldest used in mankind's religions. It was very much alive as the prophet Hosea spoke to his people in North Israel during the eighth century B.C. But it was used in several ways.

I. Death and Rebirth Among the Gods

One of the most compelling of the uses of this image of death and rebirth goes back to mankind's discovery that the earth and all within the entire cosmos are subject to death and resurrection. Mother earth produces life, but it does so in a cycle that moves from life to death to new life. The seed must die in order that the new grain may come to life out of death. The old must die that the new may live and flourish. Men and animals, insects and plants, all are participants in a cosmic process that has its origins in the very heaven above. Life itself is produced out of death. The gods in the heavens are in conflict. Death threatens life, but life triumphs over death in the changing of the heavenly seasons and movements. Men on earth participate in a great drama of death and rebirth centered in the realm of the gods.

In Hosea's day, many Israelites had turned to this religious understanding. The high god Baal ruled over the forces of life, but he was locked in a struggle with the divine powers that brought death. The summer drought came and all life threatened to disappear. Baal was gone from the scene, deep in the depths of the underworld, the realm of death. Would he arise to bring new life to earth and man? Yes, if people participated in the cosmic drama of dying and being reborn. This religious scheme is the dominant one in many religions of the world. It brings identification with the processes of nature, with the way the cosmos itself seems to move. New life comes by identification with the first time, the process by which creation came out of chaos. Back to the fount of life! That is the way to renewal. The present age is marked by decay and imminent death. There is no escape. One must die with the gods in order, with them, again to be reborn.

The theory is clear. Man is able through his worship and his ritual acts to participate in the divine drama of death and rebirth. His sacrifices, his sacred dances, his ritual battles, all reflect and participate in a cosmic drama centered in the life of the gods. The powers of the gods are not thereby controlled, but they are focused for man's good, so that man—facing death—dies and rises with the dying and rising god.

II. Seeking Death That Life May Come

Another widespread use of this image looks in the opposite direction. This present age is evil, sick, in process of dying. Life belongs to the new world that lies beyond the horizons of this world. Our job, then, is to hasten the death of the old so that the new may emerge. Man is to induce chaos so that a new order, cosmos itself, may appear. We live in a foul and corrupt world. Clear it away, sweep it clean, let the gods of destruction come to us as soon as possible so that this foul order may be cleansed in the white heat of divine wrath. Beyond the death of this world lies at least the possibility of a new world. This age must die in order that the new age may have a chance to appear.

The present scene is, on this view, analyzed much the same as on the first view. Men await life, new birth. They cannot, however, go back to the source of life and drink at its quickening fountains.

They can only, with both fear and hope, look to the future. The sooner this old world dies, the sooner new life may emerge. This is a religious orientation often called apocalyptic. Down with the old! It is sick to death. We may die with the old order, but our only hope lies in the prospect of a new birth beyond the death of this festering and decayed old world.

III. Life in the Midst of Death

The ancient Israelites and the early Christians were greatly influenced by both of these orientations. But a new dimension of understanding also emerged in the biblical world. Life and death were found to be more closely intertwined than either of the above views allowed for. Hosea spent much time telling the North Israelites that they had made a covenant with death and were ripe for destruction. He also called them to look back to the source of all life, find their identification in the love of God displayed in the past—when God delivered a band of slaves, sinners all, from bondage and set them on the road that leads to life. And he looked forward to a future in which—beyond the deadly divine judgment—new life would emerge.

But Hosea saw their present moment, which was about 725 B.C., to be polarized around death and life. The crisis in which they lived should be viewed as the birthpangs signaling new birth. Already the time of new life was at hand. The son Ephraim could not go back to some earlier epoch. He was stuck with this time. Nor could the son Ephraim clear away the rubble and thus make the new age dawn. What could he do? He could move a bit, arrange himself for a new birth, let new life happen to him. Already he was in the womb that was to release him to new life. He approached the opening. And he was reluctant to let it happen. Better this anxious existence than the unknown new perils of new life. Better to remain anxious, to thresh about, to writhe and struggle and kick and show his sensitivity to his captivity, than to make the moves that would let new birth happen. He was immobilized, not really content with letting others supply such life as he had, but unwilling to come forth to new life with the responsibilities it entailed.

But Hosea knew that his people wanted new life. They awaited it. They resisted it while wishing that they could welcome it.

How did the story turn out? Well, the Assyrians did come. They destroyed the cities of North Israel, took thousands of Israelites captive, and settled new captive peoples in the land, and the Israelite prisoners disappeared from view. But Hosea's words and thoughts did not disappear. They found a place in the life and thought of the survivors and came to enrich the religious understanding of the Judaeans. Hosea's image of Ephraim about to be born and kicking against the very thought was taken up into the Jewish-Christian heritage of faith. It has become one of the most revelatory of all Christian symbols.

But the other symbols also remain to haunt and challenge us. What do we do with the new, with new life, new possibilities of existence? We still seek them in some primordial past, and we often come to believe that the new can only come if the old order is entirely swept away. Actually, the Christian faith has taken deepest possession of all three of these approaches to new birth. In cult and worship we have a transformed view of return to the source of life among the gods. In Jesus, we say, we are enabled to die with Christ and rise with him to new life—especially summed up in the acts of baptism and Holy Communion. In the risen Lord we have the promise that the old, evil age is losing its hold upon us and the new age is being born in and around us. And in the present, we are being called to decide for life, to let new birth happen to and for us. We too are summoned not to kick against the prospect of life, not to be foolish sons and daughters, but to present ourselves at the opening of the new life.

But how hollow much of this seems to be to us! The turning back to the sources of life becomes for many Christians no more than an effort to freeze a past epoch, to make some moment in our history the substitute for primordial life with the gods. Back to the Bible! Or back to the fundamentals of the faith! Or back to the old morality! Or back to real belief in God! Such a turning-back involves no readiness to die and be reborn in the richness of the divine life. It involves a failure either to die or to live.

The other alternative always fascinates man—forward to the future! Down with the old, and on with the new! Let this world die that another may appear. Riots in our cities have shown the extent of this mood. The radical assault upon white society in the United States reveals how deeply this sentiment has penetrated our culture. Life in this society is unendurable. Let it be destroyed, then, that new life may emerge. Here too the apocalyptic vision of the Christian community is getting a hearing, although it is a partial hearing. We are on the way to a new life. The old must be swept away. The new can only come with some accompanying destruction. The prophet Hosea anticipated a radical change in Israelite society. Its corruptions had to go. Its destruction of fellowmen could not continue. Love had to triumph over hate. Pain and loss were inevitable.

Resistance to the new seems to take the form of a retreat to some old order, while welcoming the new seems often to mean the determination to destroy the present structures so that the new may come the more quickly and the more decisively. But things are not all that simple. Hosea sought to show that the past and the future had both to be claimed here and now, in the painful act of being reborn. What was really new could be resisted by those who sought to destroy all in favor of a fresh start. He did not say, "Let the Assyrians come and sweep away all the filth of this corrupt society." And what was really new could be welcomed by those who took the right backward look. He did not say, "Back to Moses! Back to the old orthodoxies."

What Hosea said was that there were signs in Israel's past that God purposed a good earth, a rich life for men on his earth, and that he would never be content with his people until that new possibility of life showed itself in them. He said that all past dealings of God with Israel, nonetheless, were only a prelude to the new that awaited them then and there. The times were evil, dangerous, desperately corrupt. But there was nowhere to hide. Hiding in the mother's womb, refusing to be reborn, was both cowardly and foolish. It could only mean death stillborn. Inviting destruction so that the slate could be wiped clean was equally cowardly. The need was for a painful birth. Nothing short of a painful birth was admissible.

And what were its consequences? They remained unclear. That is why our passage ends as it does, with a marvelously ambiguous closing word:

> Shall I ransom them from the power of Sheol?
> Shall I redeem them from Death?
> O Death, where are your plagues?
> O Sheol, where is your destruction?
> *Noham* is hid from my eyes. (Hos. 13:14)

We can translate that word as the Revised Standard Version does: "compassion." Then it would appear that Hosea threatens death: "Come on, death and destruction! Bring this evil folk to its deserved end." But we also can translate the word as "vengeance," a settling of God's score with his people, a restoring of the balance, an easing of God's wrath. In that case, God looks upon death and destruction and invites them to battle: "Come on, do your worst, you agencies of death! I am contending with you in behalf of life, of healing, of new birth."

Which is it to be? Christian faith argues for a double meaning. In the "man for others," Jesus Christ, God takes his place in the struggles for new life and does the duty of midwife. He encourages anxious and frightened Ephraim to come forth. He understands the temptation to remain hidden from life, for life, real life, is a struggle marked by torment as well as joy. He admonishes against the course of action that would destroy both mother and child. But he knows that new life also involves a kind of dying, a readiness to deal almost ruthlessly with the forces that block new birth.

Let us leave our image and speak plainly. It is too simple a choice for man to say that the source of all renewal lies in return to the past. That is not a true conservatism. It is too simple to say that the source of all renewal lies in abandoning the past and greeting the new. That is not a true liberalism. We hear about the New Morality, about the New Politics, about the New Theology and the New Hermeneutics. Their exponents are not claiming that men must wipe the slate clean, urge on the forces of destruction so that the new may appear. They *are* saying, and this is profoundly true, that we confront here and now the prospect of new and painful rebirth. They *are* saying that the trials and complexities of our present age need not lead to a wallowing in self-pity because things are so hard for us; that these trials need not issue in a decision to find some cosy retreat, marked by refusal to live in this sick and corrupt world; that our crises need not produce the hunger for apocalyptic visions of either an old world to which we return or a new world created out of the delusions of naïve politics, vision-producing drugs, or sectarian communities.

I am for the hippies who want the larger community to learn that new birth is possible for all. I am against the hippies who invite the world to go on to its destruction while they either return to the womb or make the womb a tomb.

I am for the exponents of black power who demand a new birth of human dignity here and now and who make it clear that new birth can only come about through pain and dislocations in society. I am against the black-power exponents who insist that only after we have wiped the slate clean can we hope to write of freedom and human dignity.

I am for those custodians of order who want to see the new birth of mankind marked by an easing of the pain. I am against the custodians of order—military, political, religious custodians—who are so eager for an antiseptic and painless birth that they wait too long to assist, or are so eager to see the mother survive that they kill the baby with their forceps. This latter temptation is surely a way to view the tragedy of Vietnam.

We who are gathered here know well enough what Hosea's word means for us. We have felt the stirrings of new birth. We know that it awaits us. We are right to be fearful. But new birth won't wait. God invites us to come forth. We need not be as anxious as we tend to be. The loaf and the cup provide their sustenance. The hope in the triumph of the new age over the old can sustain us. And the continuing presence of the One who presides over our new birth can be our unfailing joy throughout the course of that new life. Don't hide away. Don't just kick. Come out and live. Don't be like Ephraim. Be that true Israel whom God called.

The Plainest and Simplest Thing in the World

Albert Curry Winn

We love, because he first loved us.

—I John 4:19 (RSV)

As a young student of theology, John Wesley wanted very earnestly to be a good Christian. With his brother Charles he drew about him at Oxford a group of young men who were soon dubbed "the Holy Club." With a strenuous effort of the will, John Wesley sought to impose on himself and on his companions a Christian standard of conduct. Unfortunately, there was little peace and joy in the enterprise. John and Charles traveled across England to visit William Law, who told them that they were trying to make something complicated and burdensome out of Christianity. "Religion is the plainest and simplest thing in the world," he said. "It is just this: We love, because he first loved us."

[An ordination is, it seems to me, a time for simplification.] Can we say simply what Christianity is all about? Can we say plainly what the church is all about? Can we say clearly what the ministry is all about? Let us try.

I

"We love because he first loved us." That's what Christianity is all about. Christianity doesn't know much about God as he is in himself, wrapped in majesty and mystery. We just know how God is toward us, and that he has loved us. Christianity knows about another world before and around and after this one. But it focuses on being loved and on loving here and now. Christianity knows about law, but it insists that love fulfills all laws.

123

When our [current, perplexing] youth culture talks about caring and placards on its posters "Make Love, Not War," it is saying things that lie at the very heart of the Christian faith.

But such affirmations can end in frustration, and often do, unless the divine initiative is stressed. We can love, we must love, we do love, because he first loved us. That love is the prior source of our love. As Rudolf Bultmann once wrote, "Only he who is already loved can love, only he who has been trusted can trust, only he who has been an object of devotion can give himself."

Elmer Homrighausen tells of a newspaper reporter watching a Catholic nun mop the gangrenous wounds of a Chinese soldier. "I wouldn't do that for a million dollars," he said. "Neither would I," she quietly replied, and went on mopping. We love because he first loved us.

Christians find the clue to that prior love of God in Jesus. "In this the love of God was made manifest among us, that God sent his only Son into the world, so that we might live through him." We know that God loved us, long before we loved him, because he entered our history, came into our world, sat where we sit. The imagination, the concern, the unselfishness, the tenderness that prompts one person to stand in another's shoes, to see the world through another's eyes—that is the very essence of love. The incarnation plainly says that God loves that way: "In this is love, not that we loved God but that he loved us and sent his Son to be the expiation for our sins." In entering our history, in standing in our shoes, God does not come as the accuser, the condemner. He identifies with us in our deepest guilt. The atonement clearly says that God loves that way.

"Beloved, if God loved us that way, we also ought to love God back." That is profoundly true, but that is not how the next verse runs. God's love for us is not on a quid pro quo basis. When we seek him to love him back, he is not there. He is a hidden God. Who is there? Our brother, Sister whom God places before us in his stead! "Beloved, if God loved us that way, we also ought to love one another. No man One has ever seen God; if we love one another, God abides in our midst and his love becomes actual among us!" All those charming stories about people who waited for a visit from

Christ and were visited instead by a hungry woman, a lost child, a beggar, a leper—they are all profoundly true. "Inasmuch as you have done it unto one of the least of these my brethren, you have done it to me."

So you see how simple and how profound this Christian business is. We cannot properly love our brother unless we have first been loved by God. His love is both the source and the model for ours. And we cannot properly love God back unless we love our brother who is right here. "He who does not love his brother whom he has seen, cannot love God whom he has not seen."

II

Christianity gets embodied and institutionalized in the church. And if the church is in any measure truly the church, it is all about the same thing that Christianity is all about. It is a group of people who love each other because God first loved them. It is a group of people who are learning to stand in the shoes of others, to see through the eyes of others, to identify with the guilt of others, and not to be the accusers of one another.

It does happen. I know. In a time of deep personal tragedy, distress, and despair, I have felt a congregation of ordinary people, a church without a minister at the time, put their collective arms about me, identify with my distress. And I have known healing. I have sensed beyond doubting that the love of God, whom I have never seen, was actualized in the midst of that church.

The church's high potential for good is matched by an equally high potential for evil. It can become a center of unlove more destructive than any other institution. It is interesting to note the opposites of love in the First Epistle of John. Hatred is obvious. But sometimes unlove is called murder, or death, or closing the heart. Here in this passage it is fear. We do not love people, so we become terribly afraid of them. Fear and suspicion characterize hosts of people across the church. This is nothing but unlove.

The church has survived without a building, without a budget, without a minister. But the church cannot survive without love.

The brothers whom John mentions are primarily our fellow

Christians. This is not to limit the church to a mutual love society.
John knows well enough that the church exists for the sake of the
world and that we are bidden to love our enemies. But he also
knows that the hardest people to love are our fellow Christians.
We can do it only as we remember that all of us have first been
loved.

III

The church needs a ministry. And a true ministry is all about the
same thing that Christianity is all about and that the church is all
about. The minister who knows profoundly that he has been loved
is the facilitator, the catalyst of love between the brothers. He does
not come to give a command, but to tell a story, that God first
loved us, and to tend the results, our love for each other.

This, too, does happen. I saw a great church assembly in session under an enormous cloud of fear and suspicion—unlove. But
they elected as moderator a pastor, a facilitator, a catalyst, a man
who knew what it was to be loved, and to love. And I watched in
utter wonder and admiration as a love affair took place—a love
affair between a church assembly and its moderator. It was un-
abashed and shameless until near the end a young girl, a youth
delegate, stood up and cried, "We love you, Mr. Moderator!"—
right out in the meeting! And he replied softly into the microphone,
"I love you, too." And more important, in the midst of explosive
and diverse issues, in the midst of open and serious conflict, you
could see the members of that assembly beginning to love each
other.

High potential for good. High potential for evil. A minister
can be an agent of unlove. He can use the pulpit to project his hos-
tility against his people. He can become their accuser, spreading
death and fear throughout the church. And he can persuade himself that what he is doing is prophetic preaching. Let him learn
from the prophets. Let him feel for his people what Hosea felt for
Israel:

> How can I give you up, O Ephraim!
> How can I hand you over, O Israel! . . .

My heart recoils within me,
    my compassion grows warm and tender. (Hos. 11:8)

Let him feel what Jeremiah felt for Judah:

My grief is beyond healing,
    my heart is sick within me. . . .
For the wound of the daughter of my people is my heart
        wounded,
    I mourn, and dismay has taken hold on me. . . .
O that my head were waters,
    and my eyes a fountain of tears,
that I might weep day and night
    for the slain of the daughter of my people! (Jer. 8:18–9:1)

Let him feel what Jesus felt for Jerusalem: "O Jerusalem, Jerusalem, killing the prophets and stoning those who are sent to you! How often would I have gathered your childen together as a hen gathers her brood under her wings, and you would not!" Then he can and must preach prophetically.

There can be a great ministry with poor preaching, or with inadequate counseling, or with defective administration. But there cannot be a good ministry without love.

If I gave an ordination examination, I think I would ask two questions. First, do you know that God has loved you? Have you sensed the sweep and wonder of what happened in Jesus, that God stood in your shoes, that he did not point you out as guilty, which he had every right to do, but identified with you in your guilt? Second, are you trying to find God so you can love him back? Because if you are, you will find your people. You may go a long road, sweeping the heavens and plumbing the depths, looking for God. He is there in his transcendence, but you will not see him. He will set himself before you in the stubborn elder, the oversolicitous woman, the spoiled child. And if you know you have been loved, you will learn to love.

"Mr. Wesley, you are trying to make something burdensome and complicated out of Christianity. It is the plainest and simplest thing in the world: We love, because he first loved us."

III
LISTENERS WHO LEARNED

Air for Two Voices

Frederick Buechner

In the beginning was the Word, and the Word was with God, and the Word was God. He was in the beginning with God; all things were made through him, and without him was not anything made that was made. In him was life, and the life was the light of men. The light shines in the darkness, and the darkness has not overcome it.

There was a man sent from God, whose name was John. He came for testimony, to bear witness to the light, that all might believe through him. He was not the light, but came to bear witness to the light.

The true light that enlightens every man was coming into the world. He was in the world, and the world was made through him, yet the world knew him not. He came to his own home, and his own people received him not. But to all who received him, who believed in his name, he gave power to become children of God; who were born, not of blood nor of the will of the flesh nor of the will of man, but of God.

And the Word became flesh and dwelt among us, full of grace and truth; we have beheld his glory, glory as of the only Son from the Father. (John bore witness to him, and cried, "This was he of whom I said, 'He who comes after me ranks before me, for he was before me.'") And from his fulness have we all received, grace upon grace. For the law was given through Moses; grace and truth came through Jesus Christ. No one has ever seen God; the only Son, who is in the bosom of the Father, he has made him known.

—John 1:1–18 (RSV)

There are two voices in this extraordinary text from John. The first of them is a voice chanting, a cantor's voice, a muezzin's voice, a poet's voice, a choirboy's voice before it has changed—ghostly, virginal, remote, and cool as stone. "In the beginning was the

Word, and the Word was with God, and the Word was God. He was in the beginning with God." It is sung, not said; a hymn, not a homily. It is a hymn to perform surgery with, a heart-transplanting voice.

The second voice is insistent and over-earnest, a little nasal. It is a voice that wants to make sure, a voice that's trying hard to get everything straight. It is above all a down-to-earth voice. It keeps interrupting. This troublesome confusion about just who the Messiah was, the second voice says: not John the Baptist, certainly, whatever may have been rumored in certain circles. It is a point that cannot be made too clearly or too emphatically. It was not the Baptist. It was Jesus. Right from the beginning Jesus was without any question who it was.

"In him was life, and the life was the light of men. The light shines in darkness, and the darkness has not overcome it," the first voice sings far above all sublunary distinctions, the great Logos hymn.

And then the second voice again. Yes, it says. Only to come back to the Baptist for a moment. "He came for testimony, to bear witness to the light. He was not the light but came to bear *witness* to the light," the perspiration beading out on the upper lip, the knuckles whitening.

"And the Word became flesh and dwelt among us," the cry soars up to the great rose window, toward the Pleiades, the battlements of jasper and topaz and amethyst: "ὁ λόγος σάρξ ἡγένητο and dwelt among us full of grace and truth."

And that is true, says the second voice. The Baptist made it absolutely clear when he said—I remember the very words he used —"He who comes after me ranks before me, for he was before me." The Baptist said so himself.

It is good to have both the voices. The sound of the second voice makes it a very human sound, and you need a very human sound to get your bearings by in the midst of the first voice's unearthly music. It is also good to have the interruptions. There should be interruptions in sermons, too: the sound of a baby crying, a toilet being flushed—something to remind us of just what this flesh is that the Word became, the Word that was with God, that was God.

What it smells and sounds and tastes like, this flesh the Word buckled on like battle dress. When the Host is being raised before the altar to the tinkling of bells, it is very meet and right, if not his bounden duty, for the sexton to walk through with the vacuum cleaner. The New Testament itself is written that way: the risen Christ coming back at dawn to the Sea of Tiberias, Jesus with the mystery of life and death upon him, standing there on the beach saying, "Have you any fish?"

Have you any *fish,* for Christ's sweet sake. Precisely that. The Christ and the chowder. The Messiah and the mackerel. The Word and the flesh. The first voice and the second voice. It is what the great text is all about, of course, this mystery, this tension and scandal; and the text itself, with this antiphony of voices, is its own illustration.

Somebody has to do the vacuuming. Somebody has to keep the accounts and put out the cat. And we are grateful for these things to the second voice, which is also, of course, our own voice, puny and inexhaustible, as Faulkner said. It is a human voice. It is the only voice the universe has for speaking of itself and to itself. It is a voice with its own message, its own mystery, and it is important to be told that it was not the Baptist, it was Jesus—not that one standing there bony and strident in the Jordan, but this one with the queer north country accent, full of grace and truth. "Behold," the Baptist said, "that is the Lamb of God." Not this one but *that* one. We need to know.

But it is the first voice that prevails here and the first voice that haunts and humbles us—muezzin, cantor, Christ Church chorister —and it is a voice that haunts us at first less with what it means than with how it sounds, with the music before the message, whatever the message is; with the cadences and chords, the silences. *"Im Anfang war das Wort, und das Wort war bei Gott, und Gott war das Wort,"* the first voice incants, *"et omnia per ipsum facta sunt, et sine ipso factum est nihil quod factum est."* It hardly matters what it means at first. *"Et la Parole a été faite chair, et elle a habité parmi nous pleine de grâce et de vérité."* It hardly matters what it means any more than what the sound of the surf means, or the organ notes winging like trapped birds toward some break in the

Gothic dusk. "And from this fullness we have all received, grace upon grace, *Gnade um Gnade, gratiam pro gratia.* He was in the world," the voice sings, "yet the world knew him not, πλήρης χάριτος καὶ ἀληθείας," and *"Siehe, das ist Gottes Lamm,"* John says, *"qui ôte le péché du monde. Ecce Agnus Dei qui tollit peccatum mundi.* Behold the Lamb of God which taketh away the sin of the world."

Shout *Fire!* Cry *Havoc!* Cry *Help* or *Hallelujah, Hosanna.* A siren in the night. A trumpet at sunup. A woman singing in the rain, or a man—singing, or weeping, or yelling bloody murder. When you hear it, what happens is that the pulse quickens. It is the sound simply that stirs the heart, literally as well as figuratively stirs it. The sound of the Word sung or shouted, its music, literally makes the heart beat faster, makes the blood run quicker and hotter, which is to say the Word stirs life. Whatever it is at the level of meaning, at the level of sound, rhythm, breath, the Word has the power to stir life. And again this is both what John is saying here and what with his own words he is illustrating: that the Word stirs life even as his own words stir life, stir something. It is hard to hear this prologue read in any tongue without something inside quickening.

The Word becomes flesh. As the word of terror in the night makes the flesh crawl, as the word of desire makes the flesh burn, as other words make the scalp run cold and set the feet running, in maybe some such way this Logos Word of God becomes flesh, becomes Jesus. Jesus so responds to this Word which is God's that he himself becomes the Word, as simple and as complicated as that.

Things get into the air, we say—violence gets into the air, or hate, or panic, or joy—and we catch these things from the air or get caught up in them to the point where the violence and the joy become ours or we theirs. Peace now is in the air, for instance, and little by little we all become pacifists, and every conscience begins somewhere, somehow, to object. And the Word becoming flesh means something like that, maybe. God was in the air, and Jesus got so caught up, let this Word of God that was in the air get so under his skin, so in his hair, took it so to heart what there was of God in the air that what was in the air became who he was. He opened his mouth to answer the Word, and like air it filled his mouth.

Or God is poet, say, searching for the right word. Tries Noah, but Noah is a drinking man, and Abraham, but Abraham is a little too Mesopotamian with all those wives and whiskers. Tries Moses, but Moses himself is trying too hard, and David too handsome for his own good, and Elisha who sics the bears on the children. Tries John the Baptist with his locusts and honey, who might almost have worked except for something small but crucial like a sense of the ridiculous or a balanced diet.

Word after word God tries and then finally tries once more to say it right, to get it all into one final Word what he is and what human is and why the suffering of love is precious and how the peace of God is a tiger in the blood. And the Word that God finds— who could have guessed it? —is this one, Jesus of Nazareth, all of it coming alive at last in this life, Jesus, this implausible Jew (you let one of them in and they bring their friends—O sweet Christ, if you will only come in, come bring every friend you have if you have any friend), the Word made finally flesh in Jesus' flesh. Jesus as the *mot juste* of God.

The poetry of the first voice fleshed out in the prose of the second. The Word becoming flesh and dwelling among us, full of grace and truth, and that is not all that being flesh involves being full of, so full of that too, like the rest of us, and full of beans too, full of baloney—the scandal of the incarnation, the unimaginable kenosis and humbling of God. John means certainly no less than this, and almost certainly more.

"In the beginning," he says, "was the Word," and although it is a poem he is writing, we assume that he is being more than just poetic. "Εν ἀρχῇ," he says, and we assume he means no less than what Genesis means with בראשית, which is to say "in the beginning" quite literally: before anything yet had been made that was to be made, before whatever it was that happened to make it possible for Being to happen. You can't speak literally about such things, of course, but we assume that he is speaking seriously, as presumably astronomers and physicists must also somewhere speak seriously, about the possibility at least of a time beyond time before creation happened. At that point where everything was nothing or nothing everything, before the big bang banged or the steady state stated, when there was no up and no down, no life and no death, no here and no there, at the very beginning, John says, there was this Word which was God and through which all things were made.

The Bible is usually very unvisual and makes you want to *see* something—some image to imagine it by. "The light shines in the darkness," John says, and maybe you see an agonizing burst of light with the darkness folding back like petals, like hands. But the imagery of John is based rather on sound than on sight. It is a word you hear breathing through the unimaginable silence—a creating word, a word that calls forth, a word that stirs life and is life because it is God's word, John says, and has God in it as your words have you in them, have in them your breath and spirit and tell of who you are. Light and dark, the visual, occur in space, but sound, this Word spoken, occurs in time and starts time going. "Let there *be*," the Word comes, and then there *is*, creation *is*. Something *is*, where before there was nothing, and the morning stars sing together and all the sons of God shout for joy because sequence has begun, time has begun, a story has begun.

All of which is to say that John will stop at nothing and here at the start of his Gospel asks us to believe no less than everything. He asks us to believe that the Word that became flesh, that stood there in the moonshine asking, "Have you any fish?" was not a last-minute word and not just one word among many words, but was The Word, the primal, cosmic Word in which was life and light. All that God had from the beginning meant was here in this flesh. The secret of life and death was here.

Behold, the Lamb of God which taketh away the sin of the world. The Lamb of God approaches slowly along the riverbank. The Baptist sees him coming, and here the second voice interrupts again. Forget all this about the primal, cosmic Word, the second voice says, and about how it was in the beginning. Just watch the one who is approaching—not the Baptist there in the water. *Siehe, das ist Gottes Lamm.* His foot slips in the mud. The Baptist waits in the water up to his waist. He cannot see yet whether the one who is coming is the One he has been expecting or not. There is mud on the man's hands now where he grabbed out to keep himself from falling. Perhaps the Baptist is afraid—either afraid that the one who is coming won't be the One or afraid that he will be the One.

Mary the Mother was also afraid—a little afraid when the angel first came with his announcement, but that was the least of it. He had come so quietly, with an Easter lily in his hand. She had been wearing blue Florentine velvet at the time, with her hair hanging down her back like a girl's. Sunlight lay on the tiles like a carpet. The angel stood so still that he could have been one of the columns in the loggia where they met. She had trouble hearing what he said and afterwards thought it might have been a dream. It was not until much later that the real terror came. The real terror came when what the angel had told her would happen happened, but in a way she could never have dreamed: squatting there in the straw with her thighs wrenched apart and out of her pain dropping into the howling world something that looked like nothing so much as raw beefsteak: which was the one the angel said was to be called Holy, the Son of the Most High: which was the Word fleshed in, of all flesh, hers.

We have reason, all of us, to be among other things afraid. Like the Baptist waiting there in the river, afraid that the one who is coming along the slippery bank is after all not the One who has been awaited for so long; afraid that the one who is coming and who by now has slipped several times more and has got mud all over everything—either he is out of his head or just isn't looking where he's going—afraid that he is simply not the One at all. Afraid that he is not the Word made flesh because there was no Word in the first place and there was no first place either. In the beginning there was nothing much of anything and still isn't if you add up all there is and subtract it from all there is not. Afraid that Jesus and the Baptist meet there in the river like Laurel and Hardy, and as the water rises, their derby hats go floating off toward the Dead Sea.

Or like the Baptist afraid that the one who is coming *is* the One. Behold the Lamb of God which taketh away . . . all that is going to have to be taken away. The Lamb of God which giveth . . . God help us, the "power to become children of God," John says. Just suppose for the sake of an admittedly fantastic argument that he *is* the One who is to come, full of grace and truth and all that. Have you ever considered, have I whose trade it is to consider it ever really considered seriously, just what it is that the Lamb of God is going to have to take away?

I mean if I have any inclination at all, or you, to start being whatever in God's name it means to be "a child of God"—and let's say there is no argument for having such an inclination but just supposing that at certain unguarded moments we have it, this inclination to *start* being children of God—have we any idea at all what by the grace of God we are in all likelihood going to have to *stop* being, stop doing, stop having, stop pretending, stop smacking our lips over, stop hating, stop being scared of, stop chasing after till we're blue in the face and sick at the stomach? O God, deliver us from the Lamb of God which taketh away the sin of the world because the sin of the world is our heart's desire, our uniform, our derby hat. O Lamb of God, have mercy upon us. Christ have mercy upon us.

We have reason, all of us, to be afraid as Mary was afraid, squatting in the straw. She was afraid, I suppose, of giving birth, and why shouldn't she have been? It is by all accounts a painful, bloody, and undignified process at best. We all have reason to be among other things afraid of giving birth: the wrenching and tearing of it; the risk that we will die in giving birth; more than the risk, the certainty, that if there is going to be a kind of birth, there is first going to have to be a kind of death. One way or another, every new life born out of our old life, every flesh through which God speaks his Word, looks a little like raw beefsteak before it's through. If we are not afraid of it, then we do not know what it involves.

I imagine even, if not the fear God feels, something maybe not unlike the agony God feels as he tries to give birth to us—to make each life of flesh a word that speaks of what he is and what human is and why love is worth maybe even the pain it costs and how the peace of God is a tiger in the blood.

You can almost see the great eyes bulging, the veins standing out like ropes at the great temples, as through my cloddish and reluctant and frightened flesh, and through yours, he strains to speak again in a different tongue and to a lesser yet unimaginably significant end the Word that was once made flesh and dwelt among us, from whose fullness we have all received, grace upon grace.

Behold the Lamb of God which taketh away . . . which giveth . . . *Amen.*

The Commandment Will Not Change

David G. Buttrick

You have heard it said, "You shall love your neighbor, and hate your enemy." But I'm telling you, "Love your enemies, and pray for those who harass you, so that you may be sons of your Father in heaven. He makes sunshine for the cheap skates and the generous, and sends rain on the just and the unjust. If you only love those who love you—do you want a reward or something? Racketeers do so much! And if you bow with respect only to brothers—so what else is new? Don't atheists do as much? No, you must fulfill yourselves in love, just like your heavenly Father."

A translation of Matt. 5:43–48

Sometimes you wonder if Jesus really knew what it was like to live in the human world. Did he actually understand what people go through in the living of life? You wonder, because at times Jesus seems downright impractical, handing out commandments that no one can fulfill, like "Don't hate," "Don't lust," "Turn the other cheek," and worst of all, "Love your enemies." If he wanted to attract followers, why did he dispense such stern commands? They aren't what you'd call soft-sell. There's a church in our country with the words "Love your enemies" chipped in stone over the front door. And the minister there says of his people, "If they ever looked up, they'd never come inside." He has a point. In our kind of world "Love your enemies" sounds impossible, if not utter nonsense.

I

"Love your enemies," said Jesus. We've heard his words and we're in church; they haven't turned us away. Are the words so familiar that they no longer get to us? Or is it because, by and large, we don't think of ourselves as having enemies? We are reasonably decent, well-scrubbed Protestant people who live far from a world of personal vendettas. If we have enemies, true enemies, we can't think of them offhand. Oh yes, there are people who irritate us and neighbors with whom we disagree, business competitors and political opponents, but we wouldn't call them enemies. Perhaps in the uncivilized world of first-century Palestine men had enemies, but times have changed. We're not going to become paranoid simply to make Christ's words sound relevant. "Love your enemies," said Jesus, but the commandment doesn't seem to apply to us, does it?

Or does it? The nation we live in is a land divided; polarization is an American fact. How did Andrew Hacker put it in a recent *Newsweek* article? We can no longer be a single nation, possessed of a common spirit. "We will meet as enemies." In a way, we already do. For we all belong to groups: racial groups, religious groups, labor, management, political parties, nationalities. Within groups, we speak of ourselves as "we", and for every "we" nowadays there seems to be a "they", a "them." For blacks, there's "whitey"; for hardhats, there are "peaceniks"; for liberals, there are "reactionaries"; for conservatives, there are "radiclibs"; for Establishment types, there are those "long-haired hippies!" Living in our separate groups we feed each other's hatred with slogans and small gossip until when we meet one of "them" we feel the tension rising, the anger choking inside. Did you see the television coverage of the great peace march in Washington some months ago? Remember the faces of the people you saw (people in blue jeans and people in blue uniforms), faces contorted by hate? What was it one of the TV commentators said? "Mr. and Mrs. America, these are our faces!" Well, they are. Nowadays, when we meet, we meet as enemies.

Maybe now we can begin to understand the words of Jesus. "Love your enemies," he said. We hear his words and at once we begin to hedge: "But, Mr. Jesus, sir, don't you think the word *love* is a little strong? Wouldn't *goodwill* do just as well?" And "Mr. Jesus, sir, are there to be no exceptions in the name of national security?" "Love your enemies," said Jesus, and he meant what he said. He is not asking for a vague feeling of goodwill, because the Bible isn't much interested in feelings. After all, Jesus did not stand on Calvary and say, "I feel for you all"; he died on a cross! Love in the Bible is always more than a feeling; it is a deed, an act, a living for, a giving to, and nothing less. But still we hedge: "Mr. Jesus, sir, do you mean that we should be sending CARE packages to North Vietnam. Or that suburban Christians should work hard to house black citizens in their neighborhoods? Must every Christian 'we' work for the good of 'them'?" Answer: That's exactly what Jesus had in mind!

Donald Westlake tells of a woman whose house was being picketed by angry militants, and of how she spent hours preparing lemonade for the picketers. Apparently she had heard from someone somewhere that she ought to love her enemies. We have heard from more than someone, and still we hedge; but our questioning betrays us. We've heard. We know. "Love your enemies," said Jesus, and he meant it!

II

"Love your enemies," said Jesus. Even if he'd never spoken, we'd be confronted by the demand. For are we not the promised followers of Jesus, and did he not love his enemies? He did, and therefore we must. Listen, can we glance past the pastel pictures of Jesus patting lambs and hugging children to have another look at his life? He loved enemies. He ate and drank with rank unbelievers; welcomed uptight Pharisees; hobnobbed with hated Roman soldiers; broke bread with Judas; forgave the crowd that called him to his cross. Oh, make no mistake, Jesus was no romantic saint striding through life with a fixed smirk, like an addled Kahlil Gibran. He was a realist. He knew the Roman soldier was a vicious storm trooper; that the tax collector was a crook; that the crowd of cawing people who pushed around his cross was bloodthirsty and murderous. He had no illusions: an enemy was an enemy. Yet, he loved them all. Even if we had no commandment, we'd be stuck with Jesus Christ, the man who loved his enemies.

"Oh, but he was different," you say. "He was different and that lets us off the hook!" After all, wasn't he the Son of God, filled with God's own special brand of love? And isn't God's love utterly different from our poor, pale imitations? God makes his sun to shine on cheap skates and on generous men; his rain to fall on the just and the unjust. Not that God's indifferent, mind you. God is no great love machine strung from the stars, grinding out mindless affection for one and all alike. He knows us better than we know ourselves, sees deep darks within us we dare not peek at, and still he loves us. A Christian missionary to India has explained how hard it is to preach the love of God to people who have not heard of Jesus Christ. "To them," he says, "God's love is not only impossible, *it's immoral!*" Shall we spell it out? God loves Abbie Hoffman as much as Billy Graham; loved Malcom X as much as Albert Schweitzer; loves hard-core Communists as much as he loves hardheaded Presbyterians. Not only impossible but immoral that God should love those we call wicked as much as those we label righteous, but he does. The love of God in Jesus Christ makes him different. After all, wasn't he the Son of God? He was different, and that lets us off the hook!

Guess again: we're not off the hook. What were the words of Jesus? "Love your enemies," he said, "so that you may be *"sons of your Father in heaven."* We are to love the same way God loves, which is to say, differently. And that's where we've failed, isn't it? We white Protestant people have failed to love our enemies. We have loved Establishment people, but not those who are anti-Establishment. We have loved the well-heeled middle class and built them a billion dollars' worth of churches, but we have not loved the poor. We have loved Mr. Nixon and attended his prayer breakfasts, but we'd rather not break fiscal bread with Dr. Angela Davis, thank you. Do you know the hymn we sometimes sing in church— "They'll Know We Are Christians by Our Love"? Well, how will they know if our love is merely a little more of the same old thing? Our love must be different. Everyone loves friends: we must love our enemies.

III

So now do you begin to see what Jesus is doing? He's not laying down a commandment, he's handing out a mandate for change.

Can we obey him by going along in the same old way we've been going? No, we cannot. Somehow we've got to be different. As the old-time evangelists used to say, Brothers and Sisters, we've got to change our ways. Can we give up talking about "we" and "they" and begin to speak of all of us? Can we quit thinking in terms of friends and enemies when we are all the children of God? Listen, the Christian gospel is not a mild-mannered enjoinder to be nicer, kinder, neater, sweeter, day by day: it says we've got to be new. We've got to change. We've got to love our enemies.

Of course, it's easier said than done. Deeds of love are difficult deeds; they don't come naturally. How hard it is to force ourselves to care even a little for our enemies. We can brood over them with malignant black humor, but not love. In one of Joyce Cary's magnificant novels there's a half-mad artist who tries to sum up his faith in a sentence: "Go love," he said, "without the help of anything on earth; that's the real horsemeat." Well, it's poor advice. Unaided we'll never whip up love within ourselves, much less extend it willingly. So what's the answer? A little Jesus in our hearts? No, that won't do it. Christian faith adds up to something more than a "Jesus Turns Me On" bumper sticker and a warm-tub feeling in our hearts! Instead we must help one another in tough practical ways. We must meet to work out church strategy together, thinking through the ways and means of showing God's love. And we must exhort one another, correct one another, encourage one another, for so the Spirit works among us. Then perhaps, by God's grace, the world may well "know we are Christians by our love."

IV

"You have heard it said, 'You shall love your neighbor, and hate your enemy.' But I'm telling you, 'Love your enemies.' " We've heard the words and we are still in church. Oh yes, we hedge: "Mr. Jesus, sir, does that include Black Panthers, Communists, and hippies?" We hedge, but the commandment doesn't change. So, what's got to change? Who's got to change? Who's got to change? God help us. *Amen.*

Every Battle Isn't Armageddon

Ernest T. Campbell

> *Whosoever shall not receive you, nor hear your words, when ye depart out of that house or city, shake off the dust of your feet.*
>
> —Matt. 10:14

The term *Armageddon* appears as such but one time in the Scriptures, and that in Revelation 16:16. Etymologically *Armageddon* stems from two Hebrew words: the word *har,* which means hill, and *Megiddo,* a place in northern Palestine overlooking the plain of Esdrawlon, the site of many decisive battles in Jewish history.

In eschatology, the study of last things, the Battle of Armageddon represents the final showdown of history, in which the forces of evil will throw themselves with unrestrained fury against the good and be vanquished once and for all. The term *Armageddon* has become a form of shorthand that captures the Christian conviction that history will end not with a whimper, but with a resounding bang in which God will emerge victorious!

The Battle of Armageddon has been used by impassioned evangelists to generate leverage on the unrepentant. The term has passed over into the language and is found in virtually every form of postbiblical literature. The grim forecast of Armageddon is enough to quake the stoutest heart!

I wish to speak, however, not about the Battle of Armageddon per se, but about the "Armageddon anxiety" that crops up in history to plague man's soul in every revolutionary period.

Doomsday-criers are everywhere in our society. Population planners tell us that we had better heed their warnings—or else! Environmentalists with their grim prognostications tell us to reckon with their counsel—or else! Spokesmen for the Third World are on us to listen to their words—or else! Arms control exponents call our attention to ominous stockpiles of lethal bombs and plead with us to change our ways—or else! Alarmist auditors of the nation's morals beseech us to repent—or else!

And there are doomsday-criers in the church as well: "Update worship or you'll lose the youth!" "Stay away from controversial issues or you'll lose the affluent!" "March, picket, protest, act—or you'll lose your credibility!" "Get back to evangelism or you'll lose the world!" "Get back to the Bible or you'll lose God!"

All such ultimatums, intentionally or otherwise, induce the Armageddon anxiety. They raise conditional advice to the level of an unconditional imperative. Relatives are inflated into absolutes. One need not deny the severity of any of our problems in either church or society to observe that enough of these despairing exhortations can throw the spirit of man, even Christian man, into a state of nonproductive inertia.

There is a grossly undertreated word of Jesus' that just might help us to resist the Armageddon anxiety. It was spoken by our Lord as part of his charge to the twelve when they went out from him on their first mission. All three Synoptic Gospels report it. As given in Matthew it reads like this: "Whosoever shall not receive you, nor hear your words, when ye depart out of that house or city, shake off the dust of your feet."

John Oman calls the action here prescribed by Jesus "the sacrament of failure." It has a judgmental tone about it that puts some people off. Rabbinic law had it that if hospitality were withheld, those denied it were to shake the dust off their feet and leave.

Messrs. Major, Manson, and Wright find it virtually impossible to accept the authenticity of the passage: "We really wonder whether Jesus could have commanded this insulting gesture."

But what if Jesus instituted this symbolic act for his disciples' sake, to prevent them from falling victim to undue anxiety about the need for immediate success? John Oman warms my heart when he says, "By this sign Jesus secured his servants' peace by taking into his own keeping the success which was not theirs to command."

The more zealous we are for God, the more we tend to want instant victory. Jesus, however, graciously anticipated for his disciples, and for us, that there would be times when we would be less than invincible. Every home will not receive you. Every city will not listen to you. What then? When this happens do not get uptight. Take your leave graciously. Shake the dust off your feet and move on. Someone may come after you who will succeed where you have failed. You may do better in the next place.

The disciples remembered his words and passed them on. In the book of the Acts of the Apostles we learn that Paul and Barnabas were not royally received in Antioch in Pisidia. According to the record, "They shook the dust from their feet in defiance and went off to Iconium; but the disciples [those who stayed] were filled with joy and the Holy Spirit." "Whosoever shall not receive you, nor hear your words, when you depart out of that house or city, shake off the dust of your feet."

What does this forgotten sacrament say to us who are called upon to live in times of sweeping change and revolution? Does it not remind us, in effect, that every battle isn't Armageddon? *Every battle isn't Armageddon*!

I find here protection against fanaticism. Frequently one recalls those words of Peter Taylor Forsyth: "For the Christian nothing absolutely vital is at stake in any secular encounter." Notice, nothing *absolutely vital* is at stake in any secular encounter.

The future of the kingdom of God does not ultimately rest on human effort. That's what Jesus is saying to the twelve. If the town won't receive you—if you can't win—move on, and trust that town to me.

I need protection against the fanaticism of the one-cause man. He is legion in our society, moving everywhere with white-heat passion, reducing history to a single issue and a single solution, the one he happens to be pushing.

Sooner or later these one-cause enthusiasts commit the sin of exaggeration. They "Armageddonize" their vision. Unless this town receives *them*, unless this city responds to *their* program, it's all over. Don't let the one-cause man do that to you. The fanatic's clock is always set at 11:55 P.M.

As I catch the tenor of Scripture, Armageddon is God's show, and he hasn't turned it over to any of us to bring in or predict. The sand in the zealot's egg timer is not to be confused with the sands of history. Jesus said to his disciples, in effect, "It's not the end of everything when you fail."

Moreover, I find in this almost forgotten sacrament counsel against despair. To put it in the language of today, Jesus was saying to his disciples, "You can't win them all." It is impossible to take *Christ* too seriously, but it surely is possible to take *ourselves* too seriously. There are some situations in which we get involved as Christians that are just flat-out impossible. Bear in mind that telling word in the Gospel regarding Jesus and his ineffectiveness in one particular place. The record says simply, "He could do no mighty works there because of their unbelief." Even Jesus didn't win them all. He shook the dust off his feet as he left the city of Nazareth and went on to be effective somewhere else.

I have in mind ministers in this country whose denominations have planted them in situations that are altogether hopeless. These men are caught in the crisscross of wanting to be true while honestly trying to face up to the facts of their situation. They stay, and they stay, and they stay—because the church has not yet learned how to honorably stop something that it once honorably started! It takes faith to begin, but it takes faith to stop. It takes faith to embark, but it also takes an act of faith to terminate a journey, a program, a church, or a mission. Why is it that there are no services of worship in any of our denominational handbooks for celebrating the closing of an enterprise, the changing of a tactic, the end of the old and the beginning of the new?

This is the attractiveness of Jesus' sacrament. He is saying, "When something goes wrong and the situation will not move, don't just slink off, carrying on your back an unbearable weight of guilt! Face up to it. Cut your losses triumphantly! I anticipated such circumstances! Shake off the dust of your feet and move on!"

Sometimes we get locked into interpersonal relationships that are quite impossible. I have talked to many Christians who are laboring under an undue sense of guilt because of one or two people in their lives whom they cannot relate to affirmatively. They are bothered by relationships that they cannot actualize. The assumption is that if one is sincere enough and prays enough and is familiar enough with Dale Carnegie's book and has gone to enough T-groups, and enough encounter sessions—he ought to be able to hit it off with anybody.

I guess I am far enough away from it chronologically and geographically to say now that I was deeply disturbed on one occasion years ago because of a woman in one of my churches to whom I could not relate positively. (Have you noticed that a relationship that gets off on the wrong foot has a way of staying on the left foot in every subsequent contact?)

I found out later that this woman's father was an authoritarian type. He was about as tall as I am. Somehow, when this woman saw me she saw her father. She hated him and therefore began to hate me. I shall always be grateful for a ride in a car with a veteran of the Christian life with whom I shared my agony about this member. He said, "How did you ever come to believe that you could priest everybody? Where did you get such an idea? Don't you have other men on your staff who might help? Why not commend her to them?" He was telling me to shake the dust off my feet and move on to others with whom I might be effective. This is the weakness of buttonhole evangelism, the assumption that anybody can priest anybody else on the streets, in the subway, in the hotel—and it simply isn't true.

Bear in mind that even Paul wasn't a winner in every human relationship. Somehow he was never quite able to tie up with Demas and hold him for the faith. "Demas has forsaken me," he said. Even more like some of our predicaments was the hassle that he got into with Barnabas about John Mark, as to whether the young man should go with them on their second missionary journey. Barnabas wanted to take his cousin along. But Paul was not in favor of taking with them the very man who had deserted them in Pamphylia and refused to share in their work. According to the Jerusalem Bible, "After a violent quarrel they parted company, and Barnabas sailed off with Mark to Cyprus. Before Paul left he chose Silas to accompany him." And both teams did well on their own! Paul and Barnabas shook off the dust from their feet and recognized an impossible situation when they saw one!

Finally, there is in this forgotten sacrament a hint as to the kind of leadership that we need in every age, and especially today. I speak of leadership within the church and without. Simply put, we need a leadership that does not operate behind the mystique of infallibility. Those who head our universities, our schools, our churches, our industries, must learn when to let up and when to press on, when to pull back and when to come on strong. Next time that fellow in the office tells you to "come off it" he may be giving you good advice. Maybe you have been holding that outlook, that point of view, that way of doing, long enough!

A college president in the Midwest once told me that he managed to "lose a few" to his students every year. He did this because students warm to a president when they discover that he is human. It is hard to *love* a winner. You can *admire* one, but you rarely *love* one. The president who gets up at a convocation and backs down from something he said two weeks earlier displays the kind of flexibility that makes its mark in today's world.

Harry Truman asked us to judge him by his vetoes. Those vetoes would reveal the issues on which he chose to dig in and fight. We cannot die on every cross and Armageddonize every conviction. We have to rate our convictions as to which are negotiable and which are not.

Following the Normandy invasion Adolf Hitler was advised to allow his Seventh Army to retreat gradually toward the Seine. But *Der Fuehrer* was obsessed with the idea of maintaining a wide unbroken front. Churchill noted later that Hitler's method of fighting to the death on all fronts at once lacked the important element of selection. "Whosoever shall not receive you, nor hear your words, when ye depart out of that house or city, shake off the dust of your feet." Every battle isn't Armageddon!

I have preached to you against the grain of my own temperament, for I tend to be intense, fervent, and crusading. I have seemingly preached today against such Christian virtues as zeal and constancy. Indeed, it would appear as though I were enthroning lassitude and indifference.

I can only trust that that same Spirit who led me to this message will lead you to interpret it aright. The fact of the matter is that we are not much good to God or man until we understand that the kingdom is not *ours* to *win,* but God's to *give.* You and I are not *required* to *succeed.* We are *expected* to be *faithful!*

Boundedness: The Provincialist Capture of the Church of Our Lord and Savior Jesus Christ

Edward Farley

Jeremiah would have said we had it coming, what is happening to us. The dismissed and displaced ministers, the vacuous preaching, the clinging to the old songs and old pieties minus their power and comfort, the empty lives and despairing deaths. Amos would have said "You Know Who" was behind it. "You Know Who" was never above reducing his own shrines to rubble. Isaiah would have said he had simply pulled out ("I'll not legitimate their corruption no matter how religious their talk"). Instead of presence, absence. Instead of the light of his word—shadow, darkness, and stumbling about. "When God dies loveless hope wanders listless between tomb and temple, wishing worship, mouthing 'no' to death, singing old songs, praying as before, hiding by piety itself the Gospel news."

I

In the eyes of these ancient *nabiim,* arrested and jailed in their own time and made respectable only by the distance of centuries, that was the issue. Will Yahweh abandon us or not? The language of Yahweh's presence permeates the written expressions of the faith of Israel: God's face, his glory, his attaching his name to a place, his living in the midst of his people, his dwelling in Zion. This language reveals a very special way of thinking about God's presence. Unlike some gods Yahweh is never automatically present. He makes himself present, and therefore he can make himself absent. His presence is free and covenantal. It is also spatial: in particular locations like in a wooden box which can be carried about, a special cloud, a mountain, a door of the tent of meeting, or the Holy of Holies in the Temple. Although the faith of Israel made a large place for the individual before God in repentance, despair, doubt, or joy, these spaces of presence are not to individuals. Through the cloud, the ark, the Temple, God lived in the midst of his *people* and granted them his word of counsel and forgiveness. And this "people of God" meant something very specific: an ethnic and national people with its own language, history, land, and rulers; a bounded people, whose boundaries set them apart from other peoples (the Gentiles or "nations"). So the locations of God's presence occur in the nation. The key symbols of God's presence are nationally bounded. This people lived "before God" as a *nation*. When the nation faded and the people were dispersed, Israel remembered Zion and hoped for national restoration when God raised up the Messiah.

And then something utterly strange occurred. A religious community arose within Israel which retained Israel's faith but abandoned land and nation as setting the terms of God's presence. We search the letters and tracts of this community in vain for references to God's presence to special places. Gone are the shrines, the guiding cloud, the special mountain. More radically, we find no land, no nation, no "people of God" in the sense of an ethnic and linguistic group whose institutions mediate the presence of God. In their place we have—what? To refer to itself this community chose a term from the Greek Old Testament which simply meant "the gathering," "the assembly." In place of a national and ethnic "people of God" comes simply the gathering (*ecclesia*). At first it meant simply the local assembly of those who believed in Jesus. Eventually it came to refer to a new kind of religious community, a new corporate form of religious life centered around the crucified and raised Jesus and the preaching of salvation through him. Because the new community never abandoned the faith of Israel, it used the language of this faith to proclaim that Jesus was the anticipated Messiah. But this Messiah talk did not come easily or naturally. For the new community did not see Jesus as the One who would restore the nation to her former glory but as the One through whom salvation was now available to all nations. Hence, Jesus was almost an anti-Messiah, since he terminated the national and ethnic, the socially bounded conditions of divine presence.

What took the place of that definitive location of God's presence to his elect people symbolized by Zion? We can only say Jesus himself. In Jesus and the proclamation of Jesus, the nations (mankind) can grasp God's saving presence. Receiving that presence does not require attachment to a bounded or ethnic people with its specific religious traditions and guiding laws. No unit of human social organization is absolutely necessary for God's presence. *Ecclesia* is just as possible to the Gentiles as to Jews, to female as to male, to Rome as to Palestine, to poor as to rich. In Jesus the faith of Israel is universalized. In Jesus and his *ecclesia* all of the natural lines by which men set themselves apart from each other and along which they structure God's presence are bridged. *Ecclesia* is the one human community which can have no social, racial, national, or ethnic requirements. The very thing that makes this new community unique is the absence of boundaries and a compassionate openness toward every stranger, every person in trouble, especially the poor and the oppressed of every age, since these are the ones whom the natural types of human community would isolate and exclude. The vibrations sent forth by this new community to all strangers are clear: "The Good News pertains to everyone. Join with us and listen to it."

Human history being what it is, exclusiveness of a sort is natural and even valid. A family requires a certain privacy and isolation. A nation survives, protects its people, and serves its own self-interest by attending to its borders. A bridge club, a country club, a book club, all are bounded along social lines dictated in part by class and economic interests. We may like or dislike these kinds of boundedness, but at least closedness of a sort is necessary to and not contradictory to their existence. Boundedness of some sort is, in fact, an inevitable and legitimate feature of every human group *except ecclesia. Ecclesia* is the one form of human community which begins to destroy itself the moment it is bounded and provincialized. When a religious community turns away the stranger because he bears the marks of one of the natural human divisions (slave, peasant, black, laborer, aristocrat, hippie), it is transformed into a provincial community and loses its ecclesial character.

Lest we forget, the issue is still the issue of the presence of God. According to the gospel God himself chooses to be present in an open community, a community open where all other communities are closed. To be saved "by faith" means in part that no conceivable ethnic or cultural membership is a requirement for God's presence. "Salvation by faith" and *ecclesia* are therefore correlates. If *ecclesia* does become bounded, it ceases to be the *ecclesia* of Jesus, and courts the loss of God's presence.

II

These are hard sayings and we must try to clarify them. No human being can speak "absolutely" about the conditions of God's presence. We can make no absolute judgments about God's presence or absence outside *ecclesia*; in secular groups, in other religions, or in Judaism. We can only say that wherever God's presence is culturally bounded, it is not ecclesial presence.

We must also acknowledge that human beings are inescapably provincial. Their thoughts, emotions, and activities mirror their time and place and the forms of their boundedness. In this sense *ecclesia* itself is always provincial. It always bears the stamp of its time, place, and culture. The ecclesial community is Asian, American, Africa, rural, or urban. Ecclesial redemption permits, even encourages, deep appreciations of our home-world, our nation, our school, our family, our ethnic heritage. At the same time ecclesial redemption effects a transcending of those provincial settings. Since God alone is God, no provincial loyalty can be absolute or even primary. As the community of God's own presence, *ecclesia* itself has a primacy over other communities for those who are part of it. We cannot be Americans first and ecclesial beings second. We cannot be first of all white men or black men and secondly ecclesial men. Under the primacy of *ecclesia,* its members are impelled to view all other human beings as potentially ecclesial beings and only secondarily as members of nations, races, or social classes. In other words, they view all other beings by way of Jesus of Nazareth.

Second, ecclesial beings transcend their provincial settings, their nation and family, because of the way the presence of God in *ecclesia* addressed human evil. Provincialism itself is simply the loyalties we human beings have toward the places, groups, and languages to which we are bound, and there is nothing inherently evil about this. Yet provincial loyalties provide the immediate occasions for the seductions of human evil. Most of the horrors which human beings work on each other seem to have something to do with group pride, with patriotism gone fanatical, with racial accomplishment gone bad. If ecclesial redemption affects evil, it will affect this, and this first of all. Man, therefore, cannot be ecclesial man without his group loyalties being transcended and without his tendency to fanaticism changed. And the nature of *ecclesia* itself helps to work this alteration, for the openness of *ecclesia* to all human beings impels ecclesial people to that same openness. For these reasons, when the religious community, the congregation, appropriates the exclusiveness and provincialism of its cultural setting, its ecclesial nature is destroyed. We are familiar with white religious exclusivism. Insofar as black separatism takes over the black religious community, it risks the loss of its ecclesial nature. It is no accident, therefore, that recent black theologies find their biblical basis more in the Old Testament and the persecution of an ethnic people than in ecclesiality.

III

Little reflection is needed to realize that the Christian religion has had a very difficult time retaining its ecclesial character. Again and again Christendom strove to create a new Zion. Age after age it lusted after ever new ways of ordering the presence of God along the lines of human social differentiations. The sound of nails pounded into the hands and feet of Jesus had hardly stopped resounding when there was talk of Jewish Christians and Gentile Christians. Even though the Christian religion never conceived itself as a nation, it did erect an elaborate institution with a definitive dogma, liturgy, government, and a new geographical center, as the necessary condition for God's saving presence. The Reformation protest against this attempt to structure the salvation of God on the basis of the primacy of a geographically centered institution was an ecclesial protest. Ironically, the denominations and sects which arose in the wake of the Reformation were autonomous enough to define themselves along the lines of natural social divisions of class, race, and nation. The result has been the virtual elimination of the religious community as an open or ecclesial community.

I wish I could say that the Christian churches at the present time were merely undergoing a siege, that principalities and powers were making a massive effort to transform the churches from ecclesial communities into provincial or exclusivist communities. Alas! The siege is over, if there ever was one, and the church of our Lord is a captured church. Human beings control it who are first of all Americans, first of all white, first of all representatives of their affluent class, and only secondarily ecclesial beings. According to the reigning consensus, according to the bargain struck between the polarized groups in the church, the "openness" of the church to the stranger, the disinherited, the poor, the oppressed, the minority group, even the Third World, is to be restricted to the church boards and bureaucracies, to church higher education, and to the pronouncements of the larger church bodies temporarily gathered. The congregations are unhappy with this, and although they punish these institutions by withdrawing financial support, they live with the bargain. The congregations themselves remain closed communities, and not in the innocuous sense of simply reflecting their provincial setting, but in the destructive sense of insisting that only in their restricted social setting will they be open to God's presence. The church as a group of congregations simply mirrors the self-interests of ethnic and racial groupings. The result is not-so-subtle agreement between congregations and their leadership to keep "controversial" issues from rearing their ugly head. Since almost all of the real moral issues of our common life have to do with the crisis of our society under class and racial conflict, the effect of this censure is that the ministry to, in, and by a congregation is restricted to cultic celebration (but isolated from controversial, moral issues), the consolations of pastoral counseling, and the efficiencies of organization and church management. In short, the church congregation repudiates *ecclesia,* a form of human community in which the lines of social strata, especially those between the established and the disinherited, rich and poor, oppressor and oppressed, are crossed and a common and open community is created under the gospel. At the present time this gentlemen's agreement between congregations and their leadership is collapsing. A strong movement is aggressively at work in almost every Protestant denomination to keep the message and ministry of the church within the bounds of the cultural racist consensus, to seal off the church at all levels from controversial issues and stands. Needless to say, this effort, like past attempts to capture the church, is conducted under the slogans of "scriptural Christianity" and the "pure gospel."

We must at this point struggle hard to keep the issue before us and not let it be drowned in banalities. The issue is not tolerance, or integration, or even the possibility that the church is a society of sinners. The ordering of the religious community along racial and social lines is not just *a sin*. It is the destruction of *ecclesia,* the very thing God brought into the world through Jesus Christ as the means of his presence and the medium of his redemption. It was not simply *a sin* which Paul so passionately addressed when he wrote to the church at Galatia, but a complete reversal which would exchange everything they had won by faith for the old forms of religious community and their bondages. Our present situation is similar. It is the faith itself which is at stake, the very existence of *ecclesia* and the ecclesial community, the redemptive presence of God.

Our diagnosis, then, is not Jeremiah's. In the prophetic view God withdraws his presence from his elect nation when it falls into moral corruption. Our diagnosis is more that of Paul. God withdraws his presence from churches which abandon his precious gift of the ecclesial community. If we would account for our empty communions, our joyless and emotionless worship, our youthless congregations, we should look to our boundedness and to our insistence that God's presence be exclusive and provincial. The bounded and captured church of our Lord and Savior Jesus Christ remains in some sense the church. We can only pray and plan and fight for the restoration of that church to *ecclesia*. In that day maybe our prayers will again be genuine, our hymns joyful, our proclamation straight and honest, our consciences sensitive, our perceptions compassionate, that our lives be toward and for the stranger and our deaths be deaths in the Lord.